School Safety

School Safety

A Practical and Tactical Resource Guide for Administrators

David E. Johnson

Glenn G. Norling

Pamela M. VanHorn

Chief Jeffrey Yarbrough

Shaun Hurtado

BLOOMSBURY ACADEMIC
NEW YORK · LONDON · OXFORD · NEW DELHI · SYDNEY

BLOOMSBURY ACADEMIC
Bloomsbury Publishing Inc, 1359 Broadway, New York, NY 10018, USA
Bloomsbury Publishing Plc, 50 Bedford Square, London, WC1B 3DP, UK
Bloomsbury Publishing Ireland, 29 Earlsfort Terrace, Dublin 2, D02 AY28, Ireland

BLOOMSBURY, BLOOMSBURY ACADEMIC and the Diana logo are trademarks of
Bloomsbury Publishing Plc

First published in the United States of America 2025

Copyright © David E. Johnson, Glenn G. Norling, Pamela M. VanHorn, Shaun Hurtado,
and Chief Jeffrey Yarbrough, 2025

Cover image: © istock/StockPlanets

All rights reserved. No part of this publication may be: i) reproduced or transmitted in any form, electronic or mechanical, including photocopying, recording or by means of any information storage or retrieval system without prior permission in writing from the publishers; or ii) used or reproduced in any way for the training, development or operation of artificial intelligence (AI) technologies, including generative AI technologies. The rights holders expressly reserve this publication from the text and data mining exception as per Article 4(3) of the Digital Single Market Directive (EU) 2019/790.

Bloomsbury Publishing Inc does not have any control over, or responsibility for, any third-party websites referred to or in this book. All internet addresses given in this book were correct at the time of going to press. The author and publisher regret any inconvenience caused if addresses have changed or sites have ceased to exist, but can accept no responsibility for any such changes.

A catalog record for this book is available from the Library of Congress

ISBN: HB: 978-1-4758-7489-1
PB: 978-1-4758-7490-7
ePDF: 979-8-8818-6814-7
eBook: 978-1-4758-7491-4

Typeset by Deanta Global Publishing Services, Chennai, India
Printed and bound in the United States of America

For product safety related questions contact productsafety@bloomsbury.com.

To find out more about our authors and books visit www.bloomsbury.com and
sign up for our newsletters.

Contents

Foreword vi
Preface vii
Acronym List ix

1 The Problem 1

2 Organizational Theory, Leadership, and Management: The School-Law Enforcement Relationship 37

3 Fostering a Culture of School Safety through Positive Relationships, Communication, Student Well-being and Engaging Parents and the Community 71

4 Training for Emergencies 113

5 Communications in Crisis 131

6 Principal Leadership during School Shootings: Ensuring Safety and Support 157

7 Concluding Thoughts and Recommendations 185

Appendices 193
Appendix A: FBI School Active Shooter Incidents 2019–23 195
Appendix B: Online References (January 2025) 198
Appendix C: Training Exercise Checklist 201
Appendix D: Sample Emergency Contact List 202
Appendix E: Sample Administrator's "Go Bag" Checklist 204
Appendix F: Sample Crisis Communications Checklist 206
Appendix G: Sample Press Conference Checklist 208
Glossary 210
About the Authors 219

Foreword

Chris Grollnek

School Safety: A Practical and Tactical Resource Guide for Administrators

This unique book offers a practical and tactical resource guide for administrators and beyond. I was amazed by the details and insights provided, featuring critical strategies for school leaders and law enforcement partners. On every page, you will find professionalism and more than just the opinions of the authors, who have a cumulative experience of more than 130 years in educational leadership and law enforcement. It emphasizes the importance of strong partnerships, positive relationships, and open communication to foster a culture of safety. The book provides practical guidance on crisis communication, emergency training, and principal leadership during crises. It highlights how proactive leadership can prevent incidents and effectively respond when emergencies occur. This book is a must-read for school administrators and others dedicated to creating safe and secure school environments.

Preface

This book considers school safety, which is important and timely because incidents of targeted violence in schools in the United States are becoming common rather than rare occurrences; solid leadership is needed to effectively manage such incidents if and when they occur.

We believe this book is unique as it explains the relationships among the many challenging components of school safety and offers practical approaches to manage or address them. It is also unique by the assemblage of the skills, abilities, education, and professional experiences of the people who created it. The intended users of the book are school building principals/leaders and school district central office leaders and other professionals responsible for school safety. We, the authors, reflect a professionally diverse team with a venerable history of providing leadership, supervision, and coordination to school safety programs.

School safety has always been important. It comprises a broad variety of situations for which schools are responsible, such as planning for natural disasters, implementing anti-bullying programs, recognizing potential suicides and responding in the unfortunate case they occur, working with law enforcement, and overseeing medical emergency responses. This book illuminates the relationships among the component school safety challenges. We will address:

- Organizational theory, leadership, and management and the school-law enforcement relationship.
- How to foster a culture of school safety through positive relationships, communication, student well-being and engaging parents and the community.

- Managing communications in crisis.
- Principal leadership during crises to ensure safety and support.

School safety personnel will have different terminology, legislation, and varying resources to support them in their school safety planning depending on their location. Despite these potential differences, the general material in this book still applies from rural to urban settings. We recommend school safety personnel consider their state, and local agencies, which stand ready to assist school officials.

Although the references and sources comprising the book are authoritative, evidence-based, and/or peer-reviewed, the book is meant to be put into practice. It is a "tactical guide" for school building principals/leaders and school district central office leaders and other professionals responsible for student safety.

Acronym List

Acronym	Organization/Term
ADA	Assistant District Attorney
AFN	Access and Functional Needs
AG	Attorney General
ATF	Bureau of Alcohol, Tobacco, Firearms and Explosives
AUSA	Assistant United States Attorney
CCP	Casualty Collection Point
COOP	Continuity of Operations
CST	Civil Support Team
DA	District Attorney
DEA	Drug Enforcement Administration
DOD	Department of Defense
DOJ	Department of Justice
DRRA	Disaster Reform Recovery Act
EMAC	Emergency Management Assistance Compact
EMI	Emergency Management Institute
EOC	Emergency Operations Center
EOP	Emergency Operations Plan
ESF	Emergency Support Functions

EEI	Essential Elements of Information
FAA	Federal Aviation Administration
FBI	Federal Bureau of Investigation
FE	Functional Exercise
FERPA	Family Educational Rights and Privacy Act
FOIA	Freedom of Information Act
FSE	Full-Scale Exercise
FY	Fiscal Year
GIS	Geographic Information Systems
HSEEP	Homeland Security Exercise and Evaluation Program
IAP	Incident Action Plan
IC	Incident Command or Incident Commander
ICP	Incident Command Post
ICS	Incident Command System
INTERPOL	International Criminal Police Organization
JFO	Joint Field Office
JIC	Joint Information Center
JIS	Joint Information System
JTTF	Joint Terrorism Task Force
MAC	Multiagency Coordination
MOU	Memorandum of Understanding
NASRO	National Association of School Resource Officers
NCTC	National Counterterrorism Center
NGO	Nongovernmental Organization
NIMS	National Incident Management System
NPG	National Preparedness Goal

NRCC	National Response Coordination Center
NRF	National Response Framework
OIG	Office of the Inspector General (DOJ)
PIO	Public Information Officer
RTF	Rescue Task Force
SAC	Special Agent-In-Charge (FBI)
SLTT	State, Local, Tribal and Territorial
SRO	School Resource Officer
TTX	Tabletop Exercise
UC	Unified Command
USA	United States Attorney (DOJ)
USAOs	United States Attorneys' Offices
USC	United States Code
USMS	United States Marshals Service

1 The Problem

This chapter will introduce the background of the challenge of school safety to include trends, unresolved issues, and broad associated concerns. School principals are expected to ensure student safety at school. Hence, this chapter's examination includes an analysis of school violence, the effects of school violence on students, common characteristics of public mass shooters, the shortcomings of law enforcement, the idiosyncrasies of electronic communications and technology, schools' responsibility for student safety, the controversial and negative policy intervention termed zero-tolerance, the heightened attention given to the physical environment and hardening, whether responses and drills are effective or simply harmful, soft and hard controls and school climate, and finally the challenge of implementing evidence-based violence-prevention programs.

This chapter introduces the book and provides the core material and rationale or framework for the book's approach, which is to emphasize and offer practical approaches to address the challenge of school safety. School safety has always been important. It comprises a broad variety of situations for which schools are responsible, such as planning for natural disasters, implementing anti-bullying programs, recognizing potential suicides, and responding in the unfortunate case they occur, working with law enforcement, and overseeing medical emergency responses.

School Violence

School rampage shootings in the United States are becoming a common occurrence.[1] There were forty-eight school-associated violent deaths in the United States between July 2013 and June 2014. Victims of these deaths included students, staff, and nonstudents. Of these deaths, twelve homicide victims and eight suicide victims (42 percent) were between the ages of five and eighteen. In 2015, the rate of violent victimization for students ages 12–18 was higher at school than away from school.

During the 2017–18 school year, 70.7 percent of public schools recorded at least one violent incident. Of these, 21.3 percent were considered serious (e.g., sexual assault, rape, threats, completed physical attacks or fights with a weapon, or robbery with or without a weapon).

School violence includes interpersonal aggression such as bullying, sexual violence, fighting, and gun violence. In 2019, students ages 12–18 reported experiencing 764,600 criminal victimizations at school and 509,300 criminal victimizations away from school; around 5 percent of students ages 12–18 reported they had been afraid of an attack or harm at school.[2]

Another major category of youth violence in the United States is labeled "street violence," which differs from [school] rampage shootings by the ethnicity/race of the perpetrator, legality of the gun access, urbanicity of community, and other factors. According to Newman and Fox,[3] what sets rampage shootings apart from other forms of youth violence are three factors: (a) the location is a public space either on school property or at a school-related function; (b) shooters are a current student or recent graduate of the school; and (c) there are multiple victims or targets of the attacks.

Although rare compared to gun violence in the community, gun violence at school remains a safety concern for students, parents, school staff, and society at large. For example, in the 2017–18 school year, there were fifty-six school-associated violent deaths, which included forty-six homicides.

According to the Center for Homeland Defense and Security K–12 School Shooting Database website, there were 249 shootings in 2021, and as of May 2022 there had been 153 school shootings, defined as incidents when a gun is brandished, is fired, or a bullet hits school property for any reason, regardless of the number of victims (including zero), time, day of the week, or reason. In 2021, these shootings resulted in 168 injuries and 42 deaths. This represents more school shootings than the 1970–80 school years combined.[4]

American youth are increasingly at risk of both committing school-based violence and becoming its victims. Mass shootings in the United States have increased from five per year from 2000 to 2008 to sixteen per year from 2009 to 2013, and twenty per year from 2014 to 2015.[5]

The 2019 Youth Risk Behavior Surveillance System survey of high school students found that in the previous twelve months, 20 percent of students reported being bullied on school property, 8 percent reported being in a fight on school property, 7 percent reported being threatened or injured with a weapon, and 9 percent reported skipping school at least once due to feeling unsafe at, or on their way to, school in the past thirty days.

And gender-based violence in schools has also been increasing. Between the 2015–16 and 2017–18 school years, data from the Civil Rights Data Collection survey indicated school-based sexual violence reports increased by 55 percent.[6]

Typologies of School Violence

School violence is a complex phenomenon.[7] There is no single cause of school safety problems, whether it be illegal drug sales, possession and use of weapons, physical attacks, or theft. Consequently, no single solution exists. Failing to understand the comprehensive nature of school violence often leads to corrective measures that address only one aspect of school violence and do not stop crime from filtering into schools.[8]

School violence presents characteristics and typologies that are specific to the school context and may be different than street violence. School violence may be viewed as any behavior intended to harm—physically or emotionally—persons in school and their property (as well as school property). These distinct types of behaviors include physical violence, verbal violence, threatening acts, weapon use, damaging and stealing property, and sexual harassment.[9]

Researchers have also found that poor school-based relationships were associated with initiation of deviant behavior.[10] Many school attackers had a documented history of trouble with the school and/or law enforcement, had become disengaged from the school, and/or had been identified as troubled before a shooting.

Research on school shootings finds that attackers frequently exhibited early and immediate warning signs before the shooting.[11] The U.S. Secret Service's report *Protecting America's Schools* reviewed forty-one cases of school violence occurring between 2008 and 2017 and found that most instances of targeted school violence such as school shootings were predictable and preventable.[12]

Firearms present public health concerns at schools. Between 1994 and 2018, gun-related injuries accounted for 70 percent of fatalities in school-associated youth homicides or violent deaths; most incidents occurred in secondary or high schools and were motivated by gang-related activity or other interpersonal disputes with white male perpetrators. At U.S. high schools between 2014 and 2018, 0.5–0.8 percent of surveyed students annually reported carrying a handgun and 50 percent of surveyed high schools experienced ≥1 student carrying a gun.[13]

Effects

Such violence has a far-reaching effect, affecting the entirety of a school population, including staff and students. Whether it is experienced, witnessed, or perpetrated, school violence negatively affects the emotional and physical well-being of children and adolescents. The consequences of exposure to violence can be broader than just physical injuries. Victims are at increased risk for long-term risk behaviors such as alcohol use and suicidal ideation.

Symptoms of psychological trauma have been found among victims and witnesses of school violence. Victims often show signs of depression, anxiety, or anger. Research has also shown an association between witnessing aggression and later perpetration of violence. These consequences do not only affect the victims and perpetrators; violence also can harm bystanders' sense of safety and negatively influence the school climate for others.[14]

Studies have shown poorer scholastic achievement and school attendance, and higher dropout rates for youths attending the most violent schools.[15] Youth who experience violence tend to have worse academic and psychosocial outcomes; report higher rates of behavioral and mental health problems such as depression, substance abuse, and suicide; and are more likely to experience academic difficulties and future violence victimization and/or perpetration.[16] Psychological injuries can be sustained after direct experiences with school-based shootings.[17]

Common Characteristics of Public Mass Shooters

News media frequently profile the perpetrators of rampage shootings to provide information to the public to help explain the reasoning and motivations behind such acts. One characteristic that is prominent in these profiles is the mental health status of the perpetrators. Retrospective reports of families, peers, or teachers often describe signs of mental illness that were overlooked.[18] Educational systems are not fully prepared to identify and intervene effectively with such students.[19]

Research established some common characteristics of public mass shooters. Most obvious is that they always had access to firearms and were almost always male. In addition, a significant proportion had suicidal thoughts, mental health problems, work or school problems, unhealthy desires for fame and attention, feelings of loneliness or social isolation, and/or perceptions that they were victimized or mistreated in ways that justified their attacks.

Studies typically find evidence of mental health problems among approximately two-thirds of perpetrators, and even those figures may be underestimated, given data availability challenges. Research suggests the types of mental health problems found among public mass shooters vary dramatically, and may include mood disorders such as depression, thought disorders such as schizophrenia, and developmental disorders such as autism, depending on the case.

The U.S. Centers for Disease Control and Prevention identifies mental health problems, including depression and anxiety, as a critical public health issue among youth with significant impact on the individual, family, and community. Mental health problems that go untreated early in life are associated with further problems, including increased likelihood of academic failure, dropout, substance use, relationship conflicts, violence, and suicide.[20] A large body of theoretical and empirical research finds that the same risk and protective factors affect mental health and multiple problem behaviors, such as violence, substance use, truancy, and school dropout.[21]

On the whole, research suggests the vast majority of individuals with mental illness do not engage in violence and they are more likely to be victims of violence than offenders. A significant proportion of the U.S. population is believed to meet the criteria for mental illness at some point in their lives, but the per capita chances of becoming a public mass shooter are less than one in one million. Overall, it seems clear that even if mental illness plays some causal role in attackers' behavior by contributing to their suicidal motives, paranoia, obsession, or lack of empathy—at most, this is a partial role—and many other factors matter too.

Work and school problems may play a partial causal role in such attacks while interacting with other important variables. But most people who experience job-related stress or conflicts at school do not commit violent attacks—let alone mass murder—even if they believe they were treated unfairly. Failing in work or school can be extremely destabilizing to someone's life and personal identity, and this adversity may be especially difficult to cope with for someone who is already dealing with mental health problems.

Research suggests most public mass shooters were not prohibited from owning a firearm, and 70–80 percent of their firearms were purchased legally. Thus, such mass shooters have been able to buy firearms over the counter without the need to steal them or obtain them from the black market. Greene-Colozzi and Silva found public mass shooters often purchased their weapons from licensed gun stores, particularly independently owned federally licensed firearm dealers. In the rare cases where firearms were illegally obtained, they were most often stolen from family members.

Important differences may exist in how firearm ownership affects different types of violence. It appears firearm access increases risks of homicide and suicide. People who commit crimes like robbery or burglary while armed with a firearm are more likely to kill someone than if they did not have a gun. This suggests the firearm plays a partial causal role in their act of homicide.

Similarly, having a firearm in the home appears to increase the likelihood of suicide. Although the reason for this effect is not clear, it is at least possible that for suicidal people, knowing a firearm is within reach has a causal effect on their decision to end their lives. Even less is known about how firearm ownership affects public mass shooters. FBI data suggest most guns used in active shootings were not already possessed by the perpetrators—they were specifically obtained for their attacks; the report did not examine perpetrators' lifetime acquisition of firearms.

The role of firearms as a potential cause of public mass shootings is complex. Mass shootings cannot occur without firearms; on a societal level, increased access to firearms is associated with higher frequency of attacks. Mass shooters are significantly more common in countries with high firearm ownership rates, such as the United States. U.S. states with more permissive gun laws appear to have higher rates of mass shootings. On the other hand, it is unlikely that simply owning a firearm would make an individual want to commit mass murder. Much like people with mental illness and work or school problems, the vast majority of firearm owners are not violent or homicidal.[22]

Law Enforcement

A critique of New York City's response efforts to the events on September 11, 2001, found there was little cross-discipline coordination and no framework in place to foster or create the ad hoc organization needed to respond to such a massive event. What made the Robb Elementary School in Uvalde, Texas, attack extraordinary was not just the death toll, but that 376 law enforcement officers from local, state, and federal agencies—a force larger than the garrison that defended the Alamo—had descended upon the school in a chaotic, uncoordinated way that allowed the gunman to remain with students inside the school for seventy-seven minutes before storming into the classroom to kill him.[23]

The chief of the Uvalde school police force, Pete Arredondo, decided to treat the situation not as an active shooting but as a barricaded subject incident. He also decided to wait until a heavily armed tactical team from the U.S. Border Patrol arrived with better equipment to breach the classroom.[24] The group was devoid of clear leadership, basic communications, and sufficient urgency to take down the gunman.[25]

The response by officers in Uvalde has been broadly condemned;[26] instead of following the doctrine developed after the 1999 Columbine High School massacre, which dictates that officers immediately confront active shooters, police at Robb Elementary retreated after coming under fire and then waited for backup.[27] Yet the response has not resulted in immediate changes to how police officers are trained in Texas. Steven McCraw, the head of the Texas Department of Public Safety, said his agency would "provide proper training and guidelines for recognizing and overcoming poor command decisions at an active shooter scene."[28]

Broward County Public Schools and Marjory Stoneman Douglas High School (MSDHS) did not have an established active assailant response policy. There were no written and trained-on policies regarding Code Red and lockdown procedures.

The disastrous police response at Robb Elementary has set this mass shooting apart from others that have become a regular occurrence in U.S. life. It has renewed the debate over the role of police and cast doubt on the theory embraced by many Second Amendment advocates that "good guys with guns" are the best defense against active shooters.[29]

In an interview following the Sandy Hook tragedy, Glenn Muschert, a leading expert on school shootings, reported that the presence of armed guards at Columbine High School did little to deter the shooters and that "teaching peer mediation and conflict resolution skills" have been shown to be more effective. Similarly, Gray reported that on the day of the shooting at Marjory Stoneman Douglas High School, Broward County deputy Scot Peterson failed to engage the alleged shooter and was instead seen standing outside the school as the tragedy unfolded inside.[30]

Regarding School Resource Officers (SROs), proponents argue that they promote school safety, respond quickly to emergencies, and serve as mentors, role models, and law-related educators for students. Opponents argue that SROs damage school climate, criminalize relatively trivial student behavior, and fuel the "school-to-prison pipeline." For every heartwarming story about an SRO being hailed as a mentor or hero for thwarting a harm at a school, there are alarming accounts of SROs using excessive force—putting students in chokeholds or slamming them to the floor—or inappropriately arresting children for noncriminal disciplinary incidents better handled by a principal. The most common categories of school-based arrest are "disorderly conduct," which might be a temper tantrum, talking in class, or cursing; and "simple assault," which could be a tussle between students or something far less serious. As one scholar commented, some "children develop arrest records for acting like children."[31]

A study investigated the effectiveness of North Carolina Senate Bill 402, Section 8.36—Grants for School Resource Officers (SRO) in Elementary and Middle Schools. Seven years of data—inclusive of 110 districts and 471 middle schools—were analyzed to assess the effectiveness of the state-funded SRO program. The results indicate that offering matched SRO funds to increase policing and training was not associated with reductions in infractions per school year, which is a key measure of school safety. School size was associated with increases in reported acts, and increased grade-level proficiency was associated with reductions in reported acts.[32]

School-based police officers have not been shown to make schools safer or protect from school violence. In fact, they can undermine student success and feelings of safety by criminalizing students and destabilizing school climates. Studies show that higher arrest rates of students, especially of Black students, were associated with a police presence in schools, as were higher suspension, expulsion, and absenteeism rates. One study found a 6 percent increase in exclusionary discipline rates, with a disproportionate increase for Latino and Black students, and students from families with limited incomes, following an increase in resources for school policing programs.

Pushing students out of school through exclusionary discipline models poor conflict resolution, creates cultures of exclusion rather than inclusivity, and disconnects students from the programs and adults who may be able to help them with any underlying problems that could be manifesting as behavioral challenges.

Research also shows that students' attendance and academic performance, including high school graduation and college enrollment, can be negatively affected by police presence and increased investments in school police programs. Additionally, students can experience physical harm and trauma due to violent interactions with law enforcement officers who are able to use tasers, pepper spray, and other weapons and force; nearly 200 incidents have been tracked across the country since 2007.

A study showed the impact police contact can have on children and instances of childhood trauma. The study noted that "for many children and youth—especially those from communities of color—interactions with police and law enforcement officers constitute an 'adverse police contact,' which [is defined] as a source of physical and emotional harm that may have long-lasting effects."

This increased contact pushes students into the school-to-prison pipeline and exposes them to a host of issues that erect barriers to their success, such as grade retention, missed classroom time, contact with the juvenile and adult criminal legal systems, and attrition.[33]

National data show that Black students, in particular, are more likely than their peers to be arrested and referred to law enforcement in their schools, despite not being more likely to break school rules. In the 2017–18 school year, Black students accounted for 32 percent of reported arrests in U.S. schools, though they made up only 15 percent of the total student population.[34]

Although law enforcement presence in schools can have tremendous consequences for students, no federal SRO training and certification standards exist. Most states similarly lack SRO training and quality assurance standards.[35]

Police officers should receive intensive, specialized training before they work with youth in schools. The National Center for Mental Health Promotion and Youth Violence Prevention advises that SROs receive basic training in "how to teach, mentor, and counsel students, work collaboratively with administrators and staff, manage time in a school environment, and adhere to juvenile justice and privacy laws." SRO leaders recommend that officers receive specialized training in—among other things—mental health awareness, adolescent development and communication, implicit bias, trauma-informed care, conflict de-escalation, crisis intervention, cultural competence, and school-specific topics.[36]

The available case law demonstrates that the involvement of SROs in school discipline matters can quickly escalate these situations to include aggressive, physical confrontations and arrests for relatively minor misbehavior. Yet, 42 U.S.C. § 1983 rarely provides students with viable civil rights claims against SROs, even when the SROs' behavior seems egregious. These cases lend strong support to scholars' and advocates' concerns that the use of SROs—along with other heightened school security and punitive discipline measures—criminalizes public school students. They also demonstrate that changes in the ways SROs operate in schools are needed to protect students' rights.[37]

The lack of coordination between SROs and school administrators ranks as one of the most challenging concerns for SRO programs. A study of nineteen SRO programs conducted for the National Institute of Justice concluded, "Perhaps the single most troublesome area for most programs has been establishing productive relationships between SROs and principals and assistant principals." The study found that the underlying tension between administrators and SROs "stems from a fundamental difference in the law enforcement culture and the school culture in terms of goals, strategies, and methods."[38]

In many school districts, SROs fall under the command of the local police force rather than the school board. Some large school districts have their own dedicated police force. Even districts that have their own SRO programs have distinct supervisory structures for principals and police. SROs and administrators typically have separate professional development training and may have conflicting views of their roles. Some principals may resent the placement of armed law enforcement officers in their schools. Others may rely inappropriately on SROs to be heavy-handed enforcers of the school discipline code. The lack of coordinated training for SROs and school administrators can cause confusion when addressing conflicts on school grounds.[39]

The purpose and role of the SRO must be clearly identified to ensure a safe learning environment. Price discovered a "school-to-prison pipeline" as a result of SROs in schools. If too many students are being arrested at school, it may undermine the value of the SRO. This pipeline could reduce feelings of safety if students' misconduct is more likely to result in appearances in the juvenile justice system. Maranzano[40] stated: "Legislation is needed in all 50 states to clarify the ambiguous role police officers assigned to schools must play in the orderly and safe conduct of students in schools."

Electronic Communications and Technology

There are communication-related problems that impede law enforcement during all tragedies; such problems would include outdated or insufficient communications equipment. The hardened physical construction of school buildings can oftentimes make radio or telephone communication within the school buildings difficult (e.g., radios or cell phones that do not receive signals inside school buildings). Other communication-related problems that impede law enforcement also include lack of interoperability between the communications equipment possessed by first responder organizations and the school.[41] A critique of New York City's response to the events on September 11, 2001, found the lack of interoperable communication severely hindered response efforts.[42]

Due to the nature of large-scale mass casualty or active assailant events and the amount of first responders present on a scene, law enforcement communication interoperability problems are frequently found in such situations. Interoperability problems are magnified when agencies have separate communications systems.[43] A lack of interoperable equipment during the response to the Marjory Stoneman Douglas High School, Parkland, Florida, shooting forced law enforcement to resort to hand signals.[44]

Connecticut State Police portable radios had limited effectiveness inside Sandy Hook Elementary School, Newtown, Connecticut. In one instance a Trooper had to stand outside the building to transmit information that was being relayed to him from inside the building.[45]

Regarding electronic communications, a Texas House committee released an exhaustive account of the Uvalde, Texas, Robb Elementary School shooting listing several ways an incident commander might have helped, including noticing that radios were not working well and finding a better way to communicate. Additionally, Uvalde is around 50 miles east of the border with Mexico and is at the intersection of major highways from the border cities of Del Rio and Eagle Pass. Police had described a recent increase in "bailouts," which is when police chase a vehicle containing suspected undocumented migrants who then purposely crash and scatter to avoid apprehension. The Committee report stated, "[t]he series of bailout-related alerts led teachers and administrators to respond to all alerts with less urgency—when they heard the sound of an alert, many assumed . . . it was another bailout."

Even when there were alerts, it was not certain that everyone had received them. The emergency management alert system in Robb Elementary operated by sending out warnings online to teachers and faculty; many people accessed the warnings through a smartphone app. But not all teachers immediately received the alert about the gunman due in part to a poor wireless internet signal that made it difficult to send out the alert; also, many teachers did not have their telephones on their person or the telephones were turned off. Lastly, the principal never attempted to communicate the lockdown over the school's intercom system.[46]

Regarding the Marjory Stoneman Douglas High School tragedy, there were also no public address (PA) system speakers in school building hallways and exterior areas, which prevented effective use of the school's intercom and/or PA system to communicate the Code Red and provide directions to students and staff. The lack of an effective communication system prevented building occupants from effecting an active assailant response and moving to a place of safety.[47]

Many public K–12 schools in the United States have taken steps in recent years to tighten security. According to the National Center for Education Statistics, there are differences in the adoption of communications/technological systems based on the school's characteristics and the region of the country where it is located. Schools with greater shares of students who are racial and ethnic minorities were more likely to use threat-reporting systems and less likely to use security cameras. Panic buttons were more common in schools where relatively few students qualify for free or reduced-price lunch.[48]

The National Center for Education Statistics found that during the 2015–16 school year, 94 percent of public schools controlled access to school buildings by locking or monitoring doors during school hours. Although this approach can be useful, controlling access requires constant monitoring and a significant investment of staff time. Some school leaders, therefore, are adopting modern technologies, such as artificial intelligence (AI), machine learning, and facial recognition to manage safety systems. Instead of relying on a staff member to monitor several cameras at once for an entire school day, an AI-powered system can run on several cameras simultaneously, identifying potential threats and alerting school staff in real time.

With new technology, such as facial recognition, comes new responsibility. Thus, it is important that school principals make informed decisions about when, where, and how to implement facial recognition systems. In order to be prepared, it's important for principals to be current with new technology and continue to update their schools' crisis plans.[49]

Security technologies are not the answer to all school security problems. School districts across the country employ a wide range of technologies to prevent, respond to, and mitigate acts of violence. However, little is known about their overall use and effectiveness.

A study conducted by the RAND Corporation emphasized the need for more evidence about what works regarding school safety technology. The authors noted the need for rigorous research designs to assess the effectiveness of new technologies; they recommended testing technology in real-world settings.

A study by Johns Hopkins University (JHU) examined the technologies currently in use, how they are used, how those technologies were chosen, legal considerations, and how technology has been used in school safety applications in a sampling of countries from around the world. JHU found that integrating various technologies—including physical security, software, internal communications, monitoring, and shared information—into the school infrastructure was a challenge.

JHU also found that some schools with few incidents of school violence were very well-equipped with security technology. However, in contrast, schools with recurring crime and school violence were found to have made very little use of security technology.

The two reports observed that the recent increase in the use of security technologies by schools has not been accompanied by rigorous research into their effectiveness. Both reviews also concluded that no one technology can guarantee school security or eliminate the underlying causes of school violence. More research is needed regarding how school administrators can best select security technologies.[50]

Specifically, regarding the May 24, 2022, the Robb Elementary School, Uvalde Consolidated Independent School District, Uvalde, Texas, massacre, systemic failures—including communications failures—contributed to the disaster.[51]

Principal Mandy Gutierrez had just finished an awards ceremony and was in her office when she heard Robb Elementary Coach Yvette Silva's report over the radio that somebody had jumped over the fence and was shooting. Principal Gutierrez attempted to initiate a lockdown on the Raptor application but had difficulty making the alert because of a bad Wi-Fi signal. She did not attempt to communicate the lockdown alert over the school's intercom. She called by telephone and spoke with District Police Chief Arredondo, who told her, "shut it down Mandy, shut it down."

The Advanced Law Enforcement Rapid Response Training at Texas State University course teaches that effective communication is necessary for successful teamwork. "Regional law enforcement agencies should continually train together to establish radio protocols for use during multi-agency active shooter response." "Law Enforcement responders should be familiar with their regional communications plan but also be prepared to respond effectively without reliable radio communications." "After giving a message, [law enforcement] responders should look for confirmation that the intended party received and understood the message." "If radio communications are unreliable, it may be necessary to use runners to deliver messages." District police officers commonly carried two radios: one for the school district and another police radio that transmitted communications from various local law enforcement agencies. Although the school district radios tended to function reliably, the police radios functioned intermittently subject to where they were being used.

Upon entering the building, police officers tried but were unable to communicate using their radios. Not everyone inside the building received all the information due in part to the difficulty of maintaining radio communications within the building.

Although it would not have been necessary had responders remained focused on stopping the killing as soon as possible, as the incident dragged on, nobody tasked any law enforcement responder to establish reliable communications between the south and north sides of the building or with resources outside the building.

Based on the information developed through its investigation, the Texas House of Representatives Investigative Committee on the Robb elementary shooting preliminarily concluded:

- Poor Wi-Fi connectivity in Robb Elementary likely delayed the lockdown alert through the Raptor application. Once the alert was sent, not all teachers received it immediately for a variety of reasons including Wi-Fi coverage, whether the teacher used the Raptor phone application (as opposed to logging in through a web browser), or whether the teacher was carrying a telephone at the time.
- No one used the school intercom as another means to communicate the lockdown.
- Not all teachers received timely notice of the lockdown, including the teacher in Room 111.
- Radio communication was ineffective.[52]

Schools' Responsibility for Student Safety

Although the 1999 Columbine school shooting in Littleton, Colorado, often serves as a landmark in the public's memory, school shootings and other forms of school violence were occurring decades beforehand. School safety has long encompassed a broad spectrum of situations for which schools are responsible and go beyond firearm violence, including planning for the possibility of natural disasters, implementing anti-bullying efforts, recognizing and responding to students with suicidal behaviors, implementing protocols for working with the police and local law enforcement, and overseeing medical emergency response protocols for a range of possible health situations. School shootings have, however, become more deadly in recent years due to increased access to high-powered firearms.[53]

Some of the common responses to school shootings are not only ineffective but may also create unsafe and unwelcoming environments for students. As educators envision what they want in schools, they must also be clear about the barriers to a vision of safe and supportive schools for all young people.[54]

School principals are expected to ensure student safety at school[55] and develop plans to create a positive environment. Administrators, teachers, and other school personnel have an ethical responsibility to carefully consider the safety needs of students while they are under their supervision. Schoolchildren are highly dependent on emergency planning and evacuation decisions made by policymakers, teachers, and administrators. Schoolchildren are also dependent on the quality of the construction of their school—if evacuation routes and sheltering space within the school are adequate.[56]

In 1997 the Interstate School Leader Licensure Consortium (ISLLC) established six core standards related to effective school leadership and has subsequently revised these standards to reflect research-based best practices. The third standard reads: "A school administrator is an educational leader who promotes the success of all students by ensuring management of the organization, operations, and resources for a safe, efficient, and effective learning environment." Many states have adopted principals' license standards that are closely aligned with the ISLLC standards. These standards emphasize the need for an effective educational leader who will work to promote and maintain a safe learning environment.

A safe learning environment, by definition, is "a healthy and motivating school culture [where] [e]ducators and students feel safe, included, and ready to learn." According to the third ISLLC standard, it is the responsibility of a school's administrative team to establish and nurture a safe learning environment. However, a majority of administrators lack the training and skill set to properly address many of the issues in schools that threaten to disrupt the safe learning environment.

Although charged with promoting and maintaining a safe school environment, school officials lack the ability to do so by themselves. Dunn reported that "[s]chool officials . . . admitted that the challenges being placed before them exceeded the training or level of skills they possessed as educators." Most school administrators received training in educational and leadership concepts but did not receive training related to properly responding to an armed intruder in the building or preventing gang violence in the school's hallways. Maranzano stated, "[m]ost administrators welcome any additional resources available in the widespread attempt to prevent and respond to potential acts of violence in the school setting."[57]

Several aspects of the school context make children distinctively vulnerable during disasters. Schooling takes place in unique settings with respect to location, time of day, organization of activities, building construction, and need for student supervision. Furthermore, the adult to child ratio is much higher than in other settings—dozens of children are often under the supervision of a single teacher. Decisions school personnel and policymakers make about school safety can affect the well-being of many children during disasters.

An unexamined factor is how cognition contributes to the experience of children during disasters. It is well established that children's cognition differs from adults' cognition and that conceptualization of events and objects vary given a child's developmental stage. Younger children do not perceive threats to safety as do adults and their innate curiosity may even attract them to unusual stimuli.

During disasters, children may not be able to identify themselves or make effective decisions. Limited literacy and education levels in children may affect their understanding of dangerous situations. Children also differ cognitively from adults with respect to executive functioning—the ability to plan, monitor, and organize information—all of which will affect decision-making in emergency situations.

Children and adolescents usually rely on important adults in their environment to help them interpret uncertain or frightening situations. They also model their behavioral responses on those of adults around them in a disaster and are thus dependent on the decisions adults make in emergencies. These cognitive characteristics suggest a higher level of adult supervision is needed to support children in disaster situations.[58]

Teachers and school administrators need to be well-trained and knowledgeable about emergency procedures so they can make independent decisions in emergency situations. Teachers must decide whether to direct students to shelter-in-place or to evacuate the settings. And if evacuating, teachers must determine the best evacuation routes, give quick instructions to their students, and ensure all children are safely evacuated. Teachers and school personnel too are at risk of dying or becoming incapacitated during school disasters. Allowing schoolchildren to be undertrained and passive actors in disaster contributes to their vulnerability in disaster.[59]

Zero-Tolerance Policies

A controversial intervention in schools in the context of preventing violence involves implementing zero-tolerance policies within schools to discourage weapon and drug possession and their use on school grounds. But work by the American Psychological Association confirms such policies likely negatively affect the well-being of students without any corresponding and notable improvement in the safety of the school environment. More recent work confirmed that zero-tolerance efforts do not effectively get to the heart of the problem and cause more disruption and harm than good to students and schools.[60]

Currently, there is an overdependence on punitive and exclusionary school discipline measures, such as zero-tolerance policies, that harm and over-criminalize student behavior, particularly the actions of students with marginalized racial and ethnic identities.[61]

Zero-tolerance weapons policies are a course of action that has resulted in negative consequences. They were conceived out of the passage of the Gun Free School Act of 1994 (GFSA), are not empirically supported, are theoretically unsound, and fail to meet standardized criteria for punishment policy according to the Model Penal Code. The GFSA was a pivotal piece of legislation that forced primary and secondary school districts in the United States to adopt such policies if they wished to continue receiving federal funding. The intent was to remove weapons from the school environment and to protect students from threats, assaults, and death. The hope was to achieve these goals through policies that increased the amount of social control present in school districts by way of a so-called "get tough" approach.[62]

Punishment for a student who violates such a policy is expulsion, except if his or her expulsion would violate the Individuals with Disabilities Education Act or in the event there were extreme extenuating circumstances. In cases of extreme extenuating circumstances the GFSA allowed chief administrative officers (e.g., school personnel in charge of assigning discipline) discretion to waive the mandated expulsion of a student. Polakow-Suransky found in their examination of expulsions in Michigan school districts, "school officials often apply [the] policy in an arbitrary and capricious manner." This suggests that although chief administrative officers had discretionary power, their assignment of punishment to students was often not rationally related to the facts of the case. That lack of appropriate use of discretionary power is a principal weakness of zero-tolerance weapons policies.[63]

The Physical Environment and Hardening

There is an increasing need to consider the built or physical environment in and around schools. The built environment refers to man-made structures, features, and facilities including specific rooms, types of seating, landscaping, and stands and fences around sports fields. Some structures are used for large and crowded gatherings (e.g., gymnasiums, auditoriums, sports fields) and can become sites for violence or targets for violent attacks.[64]

In response to tragic school shootings, heightened attention has been devoted to making schools safer through the implementation of security features. Hardening school campuses by employing increasingly restrictive security technologies can be antithetical to creating open, comfortable, and engaging learning environments for a diverse student population. Excessive security measures have a negative effect on school climate, student functioning, and academic achievement. Efforts to make schools safer and more secure must also consider ways to create a school climate that is comfortable, healthy, and supportive of mental health. Thus, schools must balance students' needs for physical safety and psychological well-being by designing schools that are safe and secure, yet also welcoming and comfortable.[65]

By its nature, target hardening constitutes a particular type of threat response. Merlyn Bell and Maurice Bell[66] explain that rather than thinking through why crime happens, target hardening focuses on the probable scene of the crime and not on the possible offender. For example, how might "better locks" address factors such as mental illness, neglect, community cohesion, or pedagogical models? Clearly, when one considers the various factors contributing to school shootings that have been identified in the literature, it is apparent target hardening does nothing to address the majority of those factors.[67]

From 2009 to 2019, the percentage of students ages 12–18 who reported their school used one or more security cameras increased from 70 percent to 86 percent, and the percentage of students who reported observing the presence of security guards or police officers increased from 68 percent to 75 percent.[68]

According to Chambers,[69] the implementation of modern security technology in U.S. schools may do more harm than good, particularly when such technologies represent the primary mode of risk responsiveness. In using technological measures to reduce risk, schools may inadvertently undermine both other responses to school violence as well as key aims of schooling itself:

- Dependence on technology as a response to school violence can ultimately limit more effective approaches that are not technological.
- The more secure schools become, the more such approaches detract from teaching and learning as the main enterprise of schools.
- Surveillance measures unintentionally propagate fear in students and may inhibit healthy adolescent development.
- Security technology has a unique capacity to harmfully alter student–teacher relationships.

Surveillance measures, such as metal detectors and cameras, increased in schools that primarily serve students of color, even controlling for levels of reported crime at the school and in the surrounding community. Schools with populations comprising more than 50 percent students of color are 2–18 times more likely to use a combination of safety tactics like metal detectors, locked entrances, school police and security guards, and random security sweeps, compared to schools where students of color made up fewer than 20 percent of the student body.[70]

Schools are usually large structures, with multiple classrooms, long hallways, and big gathering spaces, thus making evacuation more complicated. The international Sendai Framework for Disaster Risk Reduction policy recognizes children across the world as disproportionately vulnerable in disasters. Such vulnerability is, in part, related to the unique physical, psychological, and cognitive characteristics of children during the developmental period.[71]

Responses and Drills

Empirical scholarship in the relationship between school security measures and school safety—both qualitative and quantitative—does not provide a consensus regarding whether security measures are effective or ineffective, helpful or harmful. In fact, for every indication that school security measures are associated with positive educational and safety outcomes, there are other data that suggest the opposite. The reality is that there is no overwhelming consensus of the research into the effectiveness and consequences of school target hardening.[72]

In attempts to prepare school personnel and students to protect themselves in the event of school shootings and to allay public fears, 96 percent of K–12 schools throughout the country have implemented active assailant protocols. Sixteen states specifically require lockdown, intruder, or active shooter drills, or a combination of the three be conducted in K–12 schools.

There is wide variation in the type of drills that are mandated and how they are implemented. The most common protocol in U.S. schools is the lockdown. The typical lockdown drill protocol includes locking the classroom door, moving students out of sight, and requiring students to remain quiet.

Multi-option approaches to active shooter incidents, such as a popular protocol called ALICE (Alert, Lockdown, Inform, Counter, Evacuate), teach students and staff to take additional actions beyond locking down, such as swarming and throwing objects at the active assailant and fleeing the situation if possible. At the most extreme end of the active shooter protocol spectrum are trainings in which first responders and actors (sometimes students) simulate school shooting events, using airsoft guns and fake blood.

Proponents of active shooter training argue that preparedness is necessary and that practice in the form of drills develops muscle memory, which enables students and school personnel to respond quickly to threats. Evidence that these drills are effective in preventing fatalities in school shootings is difficult, if not impossible, to obtain. With no empirical support for active shooter drills and the small likelihood that a mass shooting will occur in any given school, many suggest the drills are not worth the potential traumatizing impacts on students and school personnel.[73]

In February 2020, the National Education Association, the American Federation of Teachers, and Everytown for Gun Safety called on schools to take a hard look at how their active shooter drills are affecting students.[74] As these organizations explain, there is a balance between preparing staff and students and traumatizing them. The most terrifying simulations, such as those painting kids with fake wounds to simulate gunshots, may compel parents and teachers to exempt students from participating—a decision that denies students, often particularly those with special needs, access to crucial safety instruction.[75]

Soft and Hard Controls and School Climate

Brown divided most of the safety measures introduced by school officials into one of two categories: soft control and hard control. Examples of soft controls include programs aimed at teaching youth how to resolve conflict in a nonviolent manner and to avoid crime-associated problems. Hard control efforts focus on the identification and punishment of youth engaged in unsafe behaviors.[76]

There is research that suggests hard control measures have a negative effect on schools. Perumean-Chaney and Sutton referred to the "paradox of the fear of crime" and defined the paradox as "the perceived risk of victimization is often greater than the actual likelihood of a criminal victimization." This dichotomy led Gastic to conclude students' feelings and being safe at school are both important, but not always compatible, goals.[77]

Contributing to understanding the comprehensive nature of violence is the school climate. School climate includes a number of social and organizational dynamics present within the school environment that have been associated with acts of aggression and peer victimization. As such, school climate has become an important focus in school safety research and has been implicated as a critical marker of the success of preventive interventions aimed at reducing acts of aggression and promoting safe schools.[78]

An aspect of school climate is whether students feel safe at school. Black, indigenous, people of color (BIPOC) students at racially integrated schools are often subjected to discriminatory treatment, such as racist macro- and microaggressions that could lead them to feel less safe at school racially integrated schools often place BIPOC and white students into separate academic tracks, which could lead some BIPOC students to fear racial isolation and failure if they are placed in courses with white students.[79]

BIPOC students tend to be placed in less challenging courses even if their previous performance is equivalent to that of white students; less challenging tracks are associated with lower educational attainment. In previous literature on schools with majority white students, Black students often reported harmful experiences that could lead to lowered feelings of safety, such as teacher discrimination and peer exclusion. In a study of New York City middle school students, Lacoe[80] confirms that Black students' feelings of safety were correlated with racial tensions within schools.

Moreover, security measures tend to be more extensive in schools with low-income or majority-minority student populations, so the effects of increased security measures are of particular importance to the lives of youth of color. Indeed, minority-race students are disproportionately likely to attend schools that are heavily secured, even after controlling for urbanicity, family income, or neighborhood crime.[81]

The Challenge of Implementing Evidence-Based Violence-Prevention Programs

Responses to gun violence in schools across the United States have varied, but one commonality is the lack of clear, consistent plans to prevent, prepare, and react in the event of a school shooting. Gun violence in schools is a complex problem that will need to be approached with multifaceted solutions. Productive dialogue surrounding school safety and the prevention of gun violence in schools require that stakeholders fully understand laws and policies already in place, as well as the content of proposed legislation.[82]

Schools and communities encounter enormous challenges in articulating, synthesizing, and implementing all the complex aspects of a comprehensive approach to school safety. There has been limited translation of prevention science research into sustainable practices to address the underlying causes of youth violence and other problem behaviors, particularly in school settings. As a result, the effective implementation of evidence-based violence-prevention programs in schools remains an enormous challenge.[83]

According to Durlak[84] multicomponent interventions are more challenging to implement. Such interventions require effective implementation strategies to adopt the constellation of evidence-based interventions and adapt them to the needs of the context, providers, and target population. Interventions will fail to achieve their desired effects if not implemented well.

The idea of arming educators has gained popularity despite the dearth of related research.[85] On the surface, the concept may seem like a zero-cost attempt to solve the problem of gun-related violence in schools. But a detailed analysis of such a proposal raises a number of questions and highlights the uncertainties and unrealized possible expenses associated with arming educators.[86]

Many of the policies offered as solutions to the problem of violence in school spaces are created without the input of educators, without a solid research base informing these solutions, and without a thoughtful or nuanced understanding of the K–12 school system itself.[87] Indeed, many suggested strategies for preventing school violence are not empirically tested and may even be antithetical to fostering a healthy school learning environment.[88]

The tendency to zero in on certain problems as the primary—or even the sole—contributing cause has led to a fractured response both in the scholarship on school security and in the general public's actions to mitigate the threat of school shootings.[89] For example, the federal government has overwhelmed schools with thousands of recommendations for improving safety, while reactive state legislatures frantically propose hundreds of safety bills each year. In response, schools scramble to craft plans and conduct drills. The result is a hodgepodge of processes, with no clear standards for schools to follow.[90]

More dangerous than simply failing to recognize the complex causal factors involved in school shootings is the tendency of schools and the public to single out one response as sufficient. If a single way of responding becomes the definitive response to all school shootings, then other potentially useful responses will be neglected. In other words, if target hardening is the only or primary way schools respond to the problem of school violence, then other potentially valuable responses will be overlooked or dismissed.[91]

To prevent and/or mitigate violence, schools and communities must develop and implement a comprehensive school safety framework that is multifaceted, tailored to the school and community context, and involves members of the school, community, police, juvenile justice, and mental health response teams. It is important for schools to recognize and address the broad spectrum of violent behaviors occurring in schools to protect all students.[92]

It is critical to define a comprehensive approach to school safety, understand the readiness strengths and barriers to implementing evidence-based programs, and find supportive ways to build schools' motivation and capacity for overcoming the barriers to implementing such approaches. Assessing and building the readiness of schools can help address factors that may either promote or hinder the implementation of a comprehensive approach to school safety.[93]

School shootings present one of the most unsettling challenges that contemporary American schools must face, but this fact does not mean that any attempt to reduce the risk of violence in schools is warranted. Decisions to adopt specific security measures at a school, as well as determinations about the level of security needed in a school, require serious deliberation regarding not only how to make schools safer but also the possible unintended negative consequences security measures may have. The question one must address is, "what degree of risk is acceptable in schools, which aim both to protect students' lives and bodies and also to develop their minds and hearts?"[94]

Chapter Summary

This chapter introduced the background of the challenge of school safety to include trends, unresolved issues, and broad associated concerns; it provided the core material and rationale or framework for the book's approach. The chapter analyzed school violence, the effects of school violence on students, common characteristics of public mass shooters, the shortcomings of law enforcement, the idiosyncrasies of electronic communications and technology, schools' responsibility for student safety, the controversial and negative policy intervention termed zero-tolerance, the heightened attention given to the physical environment and hardening, whether responses and drills are effective or simply harmful, soft and hard controls and school climate, and finally the challenge of implementing evidence-based violence-prevention programs.

School principals are expected to ensure student safety at school and develop plans to create a positive environment. Schools and communities must develop and implement a comprehensive, multifaceted school- and community-tailored, school safety framework.

Notes

1. A. L. Whaley, "The Massacre Mentality and School Rampage Shootings in the United States: Separating Culture from Psychopathology," *Journal of Community & Applied Social Psychology*, 30 (2019). https://doi.org/10.1002/casp.2414.
2. D. L. Espelage, A. B. Woolweaver, and L. E. Robinson, "Synthesizing Knowledge on Equity and Equity-based School Safety Strategies," National Institute of Justice, 2023. NIJ.ojp.gov.
3. Whaley, "The Massacre Mentality and School Rampage Shootings in the United States."
4. Espelage, Woolweaver, and Robinson, "Synthesizing Knowledge on Equity and Equity-based School Safety Strategies."
5. B. Kingston, S. Arredondo Mattson, A. Dymnicki, E. Spier, M. Fitzgerald, K. Shipman, S. Goodrum, W. Woodward, J. Witt, K. G. Hill, and D. Elliott, "Building Schools' Readiness to Implement a Comprehensive Approach to School Safety," *Clinical Child and Family Psychology Review*, 21 (2018): 433–49. https://doi.org/10.1007/s10567-018-0264-7.
6. Espelage, Woolweaver, and Robinson, "Synthesizing Knowledge on Equity and Equity-based School Safety Strategies."
7. Espelage, Woolweaver, and Robinson, "Synthesizing Knowledge on Equity and Equity-based School Safety Strategies."
8. A. W. Dean and M. P. Leaming, "A Team Effort," *American School & University*, 70, no. 1 (1997): 36–38.
9. H. Moore, R. A. Astor, and R. Benbenishty, "A Statewide Study of School-based Victimization, Discriminatory Bullying, and Weapon Victimization by Student Homelessness Status," *National Association of Social Workers*, 43, no. 3 (September 3, 2019): 181–194.
10. A. B. Eisman, J. Heinze, A. M. Kilbourne, S. Franzen, C. Melde, and E. McGarrell, "Comprehensive Approaches to Addressing Mental Health Needs and Enhancing School Security: A Hybrid Type II Cluster Randomized Trial," *Health & Justice*, 8, no. 1 (2020). http://dx.doi.org/10.1186/s40352-020-0104-y.

11 Kingston, Arredondo Mattson, Dymnicki, Spier, Fitzgerald, Shipman, Goodrum, Woodward, Witt, Hill, and Elliott, "Building Schools' Readiness to Implement a Comprehensive Approach to School Safety."

12 Espelage, Woolweaver, and Robinson, "Synthesizing Knowledge on Equity and Equity-based School Safety Strategies."

13 J. Aggarwal, E. S. Eitland, L. N. Gonzalez, M. L. Fakeh Campbell, P. Greenberg, E. Kaplun, S. Sahili, K. Koshy, S. Rajan, and D. G. Shendell, "Built Environment Attributes and Preparedness for Potential Gun Violence at Secondary Schools," *Journal of Environmental Health*, 84, no. 4 (2021): 8–16.

14 J. L. Afkinich and S. Klumpner, "Violence Prevention Strategies and School Safety," *Journal of the Society for Social Work and Research*, 9, no. 4 (2018): 637–50.

15 D. Barzman, Y. Ni, M. Griffey, A. Bachtel, K. Lin, H. Jackson, M. Sorter, and M. DelBello, "Automated Risk Assessment for School Violence: A Pilot Study," *Psychiatric Quarterly*, 89 (2018): 817–28. https://doi.org/10.1007/s11126-018-9581-8.

16 Espelage, Woolweaver, and Robinson, "Synthesizing Knowledge on Equity and Equity-based School Safety Strategies."

17 Aggarwal, Eitland, Gonzalez, Fakeh Campbell, Greenberg, Kaplun, Sahili, Koshy, Rajan, and Shendell, "Built Environment Attributes and Preparedness for Potential Gun Violence at Secondary Schools."

18 Whaley, "The Massacre Mentality and School Rampage Shootings in the United States."

19 Kingston, Arredondo Mattson, Dymnicki, Spier, Fitzgerald, Shipman, Goodrum, Woodward, Witt, Hill, and Elliott, "Building Schools' Readiness to Implement a Comprehensive Approach to School Safety."

20 Eisman, Heinze, Kilbourne, Franzen, Melde, and McGarrell, "Comprehensive Approaches to Addressing Mental Health Needs and Enhancing School Security."

21 Kingston, Arredondo Mattson, Dymnicki, Spier, Fitzgerald, Shipman, Goodrum, Woodward, Witt, Hill, and Elliott, "Building Schools' Readiness to Implement a Comprehensive Approach to School Safety."

22 A. Lankford and J. R. Silva, "The Timing of Opportunities to Prevent Mass Shootings: A Study of Mental Health Contacts, Work and School Problems, and Firearms Acquisition," *International Review of Psychiatry*, 33, no. 7 (2021): 638–52. https://doi.org/10.1080/09540261.2021.1932440.

23 E. Sandoval, "A Year After a Massacre: What Has Changed?" *New York Times*, 2023. https://www.nytimes.com/2023/05/24/us/uvalde-shooting-fallout.html.

24 Sandoval, "A Year After a Massacre: What Has Changed?"

25　Z. Despart, "'Systemic Failures' in Uvalde Shooting Went Far Beyond Local Police, Texas House Report Details," *The Texas Tribune*, July 17, 2022. https://www.texastribune.org/2022/07/17/law-enforcement-failure-uvalde-shooting-investigation/.

26　Sandoval, "A Year After a Massacre: What Has Changed?"

27　Despart, "'Systemic Failures.'"

28　Sandoval, "A Year After a Massacre: What Has Changed?"

29　Despart, "'Systemic Failures.'"

30　A. F. Marbley, et al., "Misfire: Arming Schools with Counselors Not Guns," *Multicultural Education*, 28, nos. 3–4 (2021): 8.

31　D. Thompson Eisenberg, "School Conflict De-escalation: A Coordinated Approach for Educators and SROs," *Dispute Resolution Journal*, 74, no. 2 (2019): 29–50.

32　K. A. Anderson, "Policing and Middle School: An Evaluation of a Statewide School Resource Officer Policy," *Middle Grades Review*, 4, no. 2 (2018): 1–22.

33　M. Craven, "What Safe Schools Should Look Like for Every Student," *Intercultural Development Research Association Issue Brief*, June 15, 2022. www.idra.org.

34　Craven, "What Safe Schools Should Look Like for Every Student."

35　Thompson Eisenberg, "School Conflict De-escalation."

36　Thompson Eisenberg, "School Conflict De-escalation."

37　K. C. Wolf, "Assessing Students' Civil Rights Claims Against School Resource Officers," *Pace Law Review*, 38, no. 2 (2018). https://digitalcommons.pace.edu/plr/vol38/iss2/1.

38　Thompson Eisenberg, "School Conflict De-escalation."

39　Thompson Eisenberg, "School Conflict De-escalation."

40　S. C. Weiler and M. Cray, "Police at School: A Brief History and Current Status of School Resource Officers," *The Clearing House: A Journal of Educational Strategies, Issues and Ideas* 84 (2011): 160–3. https://doi.org/10.1080/00098655.2011.564986.

41　Federal Commission on School Safety, *Final Report*, December 18, 2018. https://www2.ed.gov/documents/school-safety/school-safety-report.pdf.

42　C. Renaud, "The Missing Piece of NIMS: Teaching Incident Commanders How to Function in the Edge of Chaos," *Homeland Security Affairs*, June 2012. https://www.hsaj.org/articles/221.

43　Marjory Stoneman Douglas High School Public Safety Commission, *Initial Report Submitted to the Governor, Speaker of the House of Representatives and*

Senate President, 2019. https://www.fdle.state.fl.us/MSDHS/CommissionReport.pdf.

44 Federal Commission on School Safety, *Final Report*.

45 Connecticut State Police, *After Action Report: Newtown Shooting Incident*, 2012. https://portal.ct.gov/-/media/DESPP/DSP/CSPAARpdf.pdf.

46 Despart, "'Systemic Failures.'"

47 Marjory Stoneman Douglas High School Public Safety Commission, *Initial Report Submitted to the Governor, Speaker of the House of Representatives and Senate President*.

48 K. Schaeffer, "US School Security Procedures Have Become More Widespread in Recent Years But Are Still Unevenly Adopted," *Pew Research Center*, July 27, 2022. https://www.pewresearch.org/short-reads/2022/07/27/u-s-school-security-procedures-have-become-more-widespread-in-recent-years-but-are-still-unevenly-adopted/.

49 M. Vance, "Looking to Technology to Enhance School Safety," *Principal Leadership*, 19, no. 9 (2019): 32–35.

50 National Institute of Justice, *A Comprehensive School Safety Framework Report to the Committees on Appropriations* (U.S. Department of Justice, Office of Justice Programs, January 2020). https://www.ojp.gov/pdffiles1/nij/255078.pdf.

51 Despart, "'Systemic Failures.'"

52 Texas House of Representatives, *Investigative Committee on the Robb Elementary Shooting: Interim Report*, July 17, 2022. https://static.texastribune.org/media/files/d005cf551ad52eea13d8753ede93320c/Uvalde%20Robb%20Shooting%20Report%20-%20Texas%20House%20Committee.pdf?_ga=2.267353038.1774615312.1696898440-306510283.1694049353.

53 S. Rajan, "School Safety and Violence: Drawing on a Public Health Approach," *International Journal of Applied Psychoanalytic Studies*, 18, no. 3 (2021): 307–18. https://doi.org/10.1002/aps.1726.

54 Craven, "What Safe Schools Should Look Like for Every Student."

55 T. C. Chan, B. Jiang, M. Chandler, R. Morris, S. Rebisz, S. Turan, Z. Shu, and S. Kpeglo, "School Principals' Self-perceptions of their Roles and Responsibilities in Six Countries," *New Waves Educational Research & Development*, 22, no. 2 (2019): 37–61.

56 L. M. Stough, D. Kang, and S. Lee, "Seven School-Related Disasters: Lessons for Policymakers and School Personnel," *Education Policy Analysis Archives*, 26, no. 100 (2018). http://dx.doi.org/10.14507/epaa.26.3698.

57 Weiler and Cray, "Police at School: A Brief History and Current Status of School Resource Officers."

58   Stough, Kang, and Lee, "Seven School-Related Disasters: Lessons for Policymakers and School Personnel."

59   Stough, Kang, and Lee, "Seven School-Related Disasters: Lessons for Policymakers and School Personnel."

60   Rajan, "School Safety and Violence: Drawing on a Public Health Approach."

61   Espelage, Woolweaver, and Robinson, "Synthesizing Knowledge on Equity and Equity-based School Safety Strategies."

62   P. Mongan and R. Walker, "'The Road to Hell Is Paved with Good Intentions': A Historical, Theoretical, and Legal Analysis of Zero-Tolerance Weapons Policies in American Schools," *Preventing School Failure*, 56, no. 4 (2012): 232–40. https://doi.org/10.1080/1045988X.2011.654366.

63   Mongan and Walker, "The Road to Hell Is Paved with Good Intentions."

64   Aggarwal, Eitland, Gonzalez, Fakeh Campbell, Greenberg, Kaplun, Sahili, Koshy, Rajan, and Shendell, "Built Environment Attributes and Preparedness for Potential Gun Violence at Secondary Schools."

65   D. Lamoreaux, and M. L. Sulkowski, "An Alternative to Fortified Schools: Using Crime Prevention Through Environmental Design (CPTED) to Balance Student Safety and Psychological Well-being," *Psychology in the Schools*, 2020. https://doi.org/10.1002/pits.22301.

66   D. Chambers, "How School Security Measures Harm Schools and Their Students," *Educational Theory*, 72, no. 2 (2022): 123–53.

67   Chambers, "How School Security Measures Harm Schools and Their Students."

68   Espelage, Woolweaver, and Robinson, "Synthesizing Knowledge on Equity and Equity-based School Safety Strategies."

69   Chambers, "How School Security Measures Harm Schools and Their Students."

70   Craven, "What Safe Schools Should Look Like for Every Student."

71   Stough, Kang, and Lee, "Seven School-Related Disasters: Lessons for Policymakers and School Personnel."

72   Chambers, "How School Security Measures Harm Schools and Their Students."

73   R. Bonanno, S. McConnaughey, and J. Mincin, "Children's Experiences with School Lockdown Drills: A Pilot Study," *National Association of Social Workers*, 2021. https://doi:10.1093/cs/cdab012.

74   D. P. Perrodin, "Ensuring School Safety Drills Meet Ethical Standards," *The Phi Delta Kappan International*, 101, no. 8 (May 2020): 72. https://www.jstor.org/stable/10.2307/26977129.

75   Perrodin, "Ensuring School Safety Drills Meet Ethical Standards."

76 S. C. Weiler, L. M. Cornelius, and J. D. Skousen, "Safety at Schools: Identifying the Costs Associated with the Necessary Safeguards for Arming Educators," *The Rural Educator*, 39 (Winter 2018): 54–8.

77 Weiler, Cornelius, and Skousen, "Safety at Schools: Identifying the Costs Associated with the Necessary Safeguards for Arming Educators."

78 A. Williford, P. J. Fite, D. Isen, and J. Poquiz, "Associations Between Peer Victimization and School Climate: The Impact of Form and the Moderating Role of Gender," *Psychology in the Schools*, 56 (2019): 1301–17. https://doi:10.1002/pits.22278.

79 S. Viano and N. Truong, "Black, Indigenous, People of Color and Feelings of Safety in School: Decomposing Variation and Ecological Assets," *AERA Open*, 8 (2022). https://doi.org/10.1177/23328584221138484.

80 Viano and Truong, "Black, Indigenous, People of Color and Feelings of Safety in School."

81 Chambers, "How School Security Measures Harm Schools and their Students."

82 L. Isbell, K. Dixon, and A. Sanders, "Arming Teachers for School Safety: Providing Clarity for State Policies," *Texas Education Review*, 7, no. 2 (2019): 6–13.

83 Kingston, Arredondo Mattson, Dymnicki, Spier, Fitzgerald, Shipman, Goodrum, Woodward, Witt, Hill, and Elliott, "Building Schools' Readiness to Implement a Comprehensive Approach to School Safety."

84 Eisman, Heinze, Kilbourne, Franzen, Melde, and McGarrell, "Comprehensive Approaches to Addressing Mental Health Needs and Enhancing School Security."

85 Weiler and Cray, "Police at School: A Brief History and Current Status of School Resource Officers."

86 Weiler and Cray, "Police at School: A Brief History and Current Status of School Resource Officers."

87 Rajan, "School Safety and Violence: Drawing on a Public Health Approach."

88 Lamoreaux and Sulkowski, "An Alternative to Fortified Schools."

89 Chambers, "How School Security Measures Harm Schools and Their Students."

90 Perrodin, "Ensuring School Safety Drills Meet Ethical Standards."

91 Chambers, "How School Security Measures Harm Schools and their Students."

92 Espelage, Woolweaver, and Robinson, "Synthesizing Knowledge on Equity and Equity-based School Safety Strategies."

93 Kingston, Arredondo Mattson, Dymnicki, Spier, Fitzgerald, Shipman, Goodrum, Woodward, Witt, Hill, and Elliott, "Building Schools' Readiness to Implement a Comprehensive Approach to School Safety."

Bibliography

Afkinich, J. L., and S. Klumpner (2018). "Violence Prevention Strategies and School Safety." *Journal of the Society for Social Work and Research*, 9(4): 637–50.

Aggarwal, J., E. S. Eitland, L. N. Gonzalez, M. L. Fakeh Campbell, P. Greenberg, E. Kaplun, S. Sahili, K. Koshy, S. Rajan, D. G. Shendell, "Built Environment Attributes and Preparedness for Potential Gun Violence at Secondary Schools." *Journal of Environmental Health*, 84, no. 4 (November 2021): 8–16.

Anderson, K. A. "Policing and Middle School: An Evaluation of a Statewide School Resource Officer Policy." *Middle Grades Review*, 4, no. 2 (2018): 1–22.

Barzman, D., Y. Ni, M. Griffey, A. Bachtel, K. Lin, H. Jackson, M. Sorter, and M. DelBello. "Automated Risk Assessment for School Violence: A Pilot Study." *Psychiatric Quarterly*, 89 (2018): 817–28. https://doi.org/10.1007/s11126-018-9581-8.

Bonanno, R., S. McConnaughey, and J. Mincin. "Children's Experiences with School Lockdown Drills: A Pilot Study." *National Association of Social Workers*, 2021. https://doi:10.1093/cs/cdab012.

Chambers, D. "How School Security Measures Harm Schools and Their Students." *Educational Theory*, 72, no. 2 (2022): 123–53.

Chan, T. C., B. Jiang, M. Chandler, R. Morris, S. Rebisz, S. Turan, Z. Shu, and S. Kpeglo. "School Principals' Self-perceptions of Their Roles and Responsibilities in Six Countries." *New Waves Educational Research & Development*, 22, no. 2 (2019): 37–61.

Connecticut State Police. *After Action Report: Newtown Shooting Incident*, 2012. https://portal.ct.gov/-/media/DESPP/DSP/CSPAARpdf.pdf.

Craven, M. "What Safe Schools Should Look Like for Every Student." *Intercultural Development Research Association Issue Brief*, June 15, 2022. www.idra.org

Dean, A. W., and M. P. Leaming. "A Team Effort." *American School & University*, 70, no. 1 (1997): 181–194.

Despart, Z. "'Systemic Failures' in Uvalde Shooting Went Far Beyond Local Police, Texas House Report Details." *The Texas Tribune*, July 17, 2022. https://www.texastribune.org/2022/07/17/law-enforcement-failure-uvalde-shooting-investigation/.

Eisman, A. B., J. Heinze, A. M. Kilbourne, S. Franzen, C. Melde, and E. McGarrell. "Comprehensive Approaches to Addressing Mental Health Needs and Enhancing

School Security: A Hybrid Type II Cluster Randomized Trial." *Health & Justice*, 8, no. 1 (2020). http://dx.doi.org/10.1186/s40352-020-0104-y.

Espelage, D. L., A. B. Woolweaver, and L. E. Robinson. "Synthesizing Knowledge on Equity and Equity-based School Safety Strategies." National Institute of Justice, 2023. NIJ.ojp.gov.

Federal Commission on School Safety. *Final Report,* December 18, 2018. https://www2.ed.gov/documents/school-safety/school-safety-report.pdf.

Isbell, L., K. Dixon, and A. Sanders. "Arming Teachers for School Safety: Providing Clarity for State Policies." *Texas Education Review*, 7, no. 2 (2019): 6–13.

Kingston, B., S. Arredondo Mattson, A. Dymnicki, E. Spier, M. Fitzgerald, K. Shipman, S. Goodrum, W. Woodward, J. Witt, K. G. Hill, and D. Elliott. "Building Schools' Readiness to Implement a Comprehensive Approach to School Safety." *Clinical Child and Family Psychology Review*, 21 (2018): 433–49. https://doi.org/10.1007/s10567-018-0264-7.

Lamoreaux, D., and M. L. Sulkowski. "An Alternative to Fortified Schools: Using Crime Prevention Through Environmental Design (CPTED) to Balance Student Safety and Psychological Well-being." *Psychology in the Schools*, 2020. https://doi.org/10.1002/pits.22301.

Lankford, A., and J. R. Silva. "The Timing of Opportunities to Prevent Mass Shootings: A Study of Mental Health Contacts, Work and School Problems, and Firearms Acquisition." *International Review of Psychiatry*, 33, no. 7 (2021): 638–52. https://doi.org/10.1080/09540261.2021.1932440.

Marbley, A. F. et al. "Misfire: Arming Schools with Counselors Not Guns." *Multicultural Education*, 28, nos. 3–4 (2021): 8.

Marjory Stoneman Douglas High School Public Safety Commission. *Initial Report Submitted to the Governor, Speaker of the House of Representatives and Senate President*, 2019. https://www.fdle.state.fl.us/MSDHS/CommissionReport.pdf.

Mongan, P., and R. Walker. "'The Road to Hell Is Paved with Good Intentions': A Historical, Theoretical, and Legal Analysis of Zero-Tolerance Weapons Policies in American Schools." *Preventing School Failure*, 56, no. 4 (2012): 232–40. https://doi.org/10.1080/1045988X.2011.654366.

Moore, H., R. A. Astor, and R. Benbenishty. "A Statewide Study of School-based Victimization, Discriminatory Bullying, and Weapon Victimization by Student Homelessness Status." *National Association of Social Workers*, 43, no. 3 (2019): 181–194.

National Institute of Justice. *A Comprehensive School Safety Framework Report to the Committees on Appropriations* (U.S. Department of Justice, Office of Justice Programs, 2020). https://www.ojp.gov/pdffiles1/nij/255078.pdf.

Perrodin, D. P. "Ensuring School Safety Drills Meet Ethical Standards." *The Phi Delta Kappan International*, 101, no. 8 (2020): 72. https://www.jstor.org/stable/10.2307/26977129.

Rajan, S. "School Safety and Violence: Drawing on a Public Health Approach." *International Journal of Applied Psychoanalytic Studies*, 18, no. 3 (2021): 307–18. https://doi.org/10.1002/aps.1726.

Renaud, C. "The Missing Piece of NIMS: Teaching Incident Commanders How to Function in the Edge of Chaos." *Homeland Security Affairs*, 2012. https://www.hsaj.org/articles/221.

Sandoval, E. "A Year After a Massacre: What Has Changed?" *New York Times*, May 25, 2023. https://www.nytimes.com/2023/05/24/us/uvalde-shooting-fallout.html.

Schaeffer, K. "US School Security Procedures Have become More Widespread in Recent Years But Are Still Unevenly Adopted." *Pew Research Center*, July 27, 2022. https://www.pewresearch.org/short-reads/2022/07/27/u-s-school-security-procedures-have-become-more-widespread-in-recent-years-but-are-still-unevenly-adopted/.

Stough, L. M., D. Kang, and S. Lee. "Seven School-Related Disasters: Lessons for Policymakers and School Personnel." *Education Policy Analysis Archives*, 26, no. 100 (2018). http://dx.doi.org/10.14507/epaa.26.3698.

Texas House of Representatives. *Investigative Committee on the Robb Elementary Shooting: Interim Report*, July 17, 2022. https://static.texastribune.org/media/files/d005cf551ad52eea13d8753ede93320c/Uvalde%20Robb%20Shooting%20Report%20-%20Texas%20House%20Committee.pdf?_ga=2.267353038.1774615312.1696898440-306510283.1694049353.

Thompson Eisenberg, D. "School Conflict De-escalation: A Coordinated Approach for Educators and SROs." *Dispute Resolution Journal*, 74, no. 2 (2019): 29–50.

Vance, M. "Looking to Technology to Enhance School Safety." *Principal Leadership*, 19, no. 9 (2019): 32–35.

Viano, S., and N. Truong, "Black, Indigenous, People of Color and Feelings of Safety in School: Decomposing Variation and Ecological Assets." *AERA Open*, 8 (2022). https://doi.org/10.1177/23328584221138484.

Weiler, S. C., L. M. Cornelius, and J. D. Skousen. "Safety at Schools: Identifying the Costs Associated with the Necessary Safeguards for Arming Educators." *The Rural Educator*, 39 (2018): 54–58.

Weiler, S. C., and M. Cray, "Police at School: A Brief History and Current Status of School Resource Officers." *The Clearing House: A Journal of Educational Strategies, Issues and Ideas*, 84 (2011): 160–3. https://doi.org/10.1080/00098655.2011.564986.

Whaley, A. L. "The Massacre Mentality and School Rampage Shootings in the United States: Separating Culture from Psychopathology." *Journal of Community & Applied Social Psychology*, 30 (2019). https://doi.org/10.1002/casp.2414.

Williford, A., P. J. Fite, D. Isen, and J. Poquiz, "Associations between Peer Victimization and School Climate: The Impact of Form and the Moderating Role of Gender." *Psychology in the Schools*, 56 (2019): 1301–17. https://doi:10.1002/pits.22278.

Wolf, K. C. "Assessing Students' Civil Rights Claims Against School Resource Officers." *Pace Law Review*, 38, no. 2 (2018). https://digitalcommons.pace.edu/plr/vol38/iss2/1.

2 Organizational Theory, Leadership, and Management

The School-Law Enforcement Relationship

The landscape of school safety and policing in the United States has undergone significant transformation in the twenty-first century, primarily due to the rise in active attack and shooter events on educational campuses. Public schools and institutions of higher education have actively explored efficient and sustainable solutions aimed at bolstering critical incident management. Effective solutions have a common theme which encompasses various facets related to prevention, mitigation, preparedness, response, and recovery. Strategies developed to address such challenges include the implementation of standardized response protocols, integration of modern safety, and security technologies, the development of safety measures designed to fortify buildings, and the deployment of trained police officers tasked with safeguarding students, staff, and the overall campus environment.

True school safety and security requires a multilayered approach that demands commitment and consistent collaboration between law enforcement and educators. Cultural shifts in the methods used require transformative school policing leadership and student advocacy practices that embrace alternative solutions to the criminal justice system.

The Origin of Police in Schools

While there are benefits to having police on campuses, the introduction of armed officers to educational institutions has raised concerns for some who consider police in schools to be an unwelcome addition. A primary argument raised is a resulting increase in negative interactions between police and students, especially in situations involving noncriminal, reckless, or juvenile behavior. Critics argue that such interactions may lead to negative outcomes, particularly impacting students from historically marginalized groups. Disparate outcomes remain a point of emphasis among those concerned about increased police presence in schools.

For generations, law enforcement agencies in the United States have been tasked with addressing issues related to the criminal behavior of young adults and the resulting challenges of juvenile delinquency. A prevalent approach within policing involves referring delinquent conduct cases to juvenile services and juvenile courts as the primary avenue for intervention and resolution. The inception of school policing was not in response to escalating school violence. Instead, it traces back to a pioneering initiative that began in Flint, Michigan, during the 1950s as a positive student development effort. It marked the first official act of using contracted police services in a public school setting.[1]

This pioneering effort was aimed at establishing a Police-School Liaison program, which eventually evolved into what is commonly known today as the School Resource Officer (SRO) program. The innovative approach presented a unique opportunity for local law enforcement to collaborate with community schools, striving to foster improved relationships between police officers and students while cultivating safe and conducive learning environments. The success and positive outcomes of the Flint, Michigan, project served as a blueprint for the development and implementation of school policing initiatives across the nation.

There is a notable expansion of school police officer programs within public schools throughout the United States. According to the National Center for Education Statistics (NCES), as of 2021, the estimated count of law enforcement officers stationed in schools exceeded 20,000.[2]

Given the substantial increase in school violence and active shooter incidents in the twenty-first century, educational institutions have increasingly adopted school safety measures that involve the incorporation of school police officers.

The transition toward school districts establishing their own school district police departments in the United States has been somewhat of a reluctant evolution. Many district administrators and parents resisted the approach for a variety of reasons, including the perception of having police officers on campus sent regarding the true safety of a campus. A historical argument made was that if a school district was safe, why is there a need for police? The emergent reality of today is that even the safest schools are subject to unpredictable attacks by individuals with ill-intent. In response, school districts have deployed multilayered school safety solutions, including adding armed police officers to campuses.

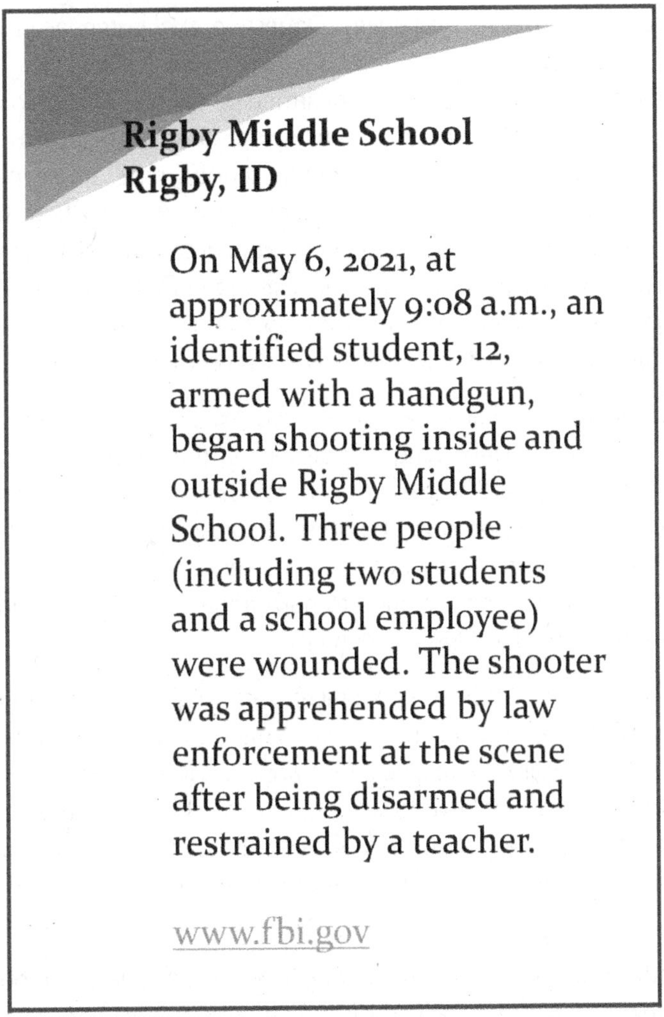

> **Rigby Middle School**
> **Rigby, ID**
>
> On May 6, 2021, at approximately 9:08 a.m., an identified student, 12, armed with a handgun, began shooting inside and outside Rigby Middle School. Three people (including two students and a school employee) were wounded. The shooter was apprehended by law enforcement at the scene after being disarmed and restrained by a teacher.
>
> www.fbi.gov

Figure 2.1. Rigby Middle School, Idaho. www.fbi.gov

Quality vs Convenience in School-Based Policing

Districts that seek to create their own police departments cite incentives such as the ability to exert better control over the quality, training, and responsibilities of police officers serving students and schools. As of January 2023, more than 300 out of the 1,029 public school districts in Texas had their own school district police departments.[3]

The increased expansion of school district police departments and police presence in schools has called into question the potential increase of students entering the criminal justice system. Several states have enacted legislation mandating the presence of armed personnel or police officers on school campuses. During the Texas 88th legislature in 2023, House Bill 3 (HB3) was passed which mandated that public schools have armed personnel on each campus. In response, many school districts established their own police departments. Additional benefits highlighted included heightened visibility to discourage criminal activity, expanded foot and vehicle patrols, investigations of on-campus criminal offenses, and proactive threat response that reaffirm to stakeholders a school district's commitment to student safety.

A predominant societal expectation revolves around the adoption of measures aimed at establishing and preserving the safest and most secure learning environments. These expectations exist from national to local levels, encompassing neighborhoods, businesses, places of worship, and schools. Parents expect that the presence of police services within school settings will provide a positive contribution to nurturing spaces where children can flourish without the looming fear of harm.

School-based law enforcement officers are highly trained experts in maintaining peace and security for students and staff. In an educational setting, officers facilitate effective interactions and interventions that include enhancing relationships beyond school campuses. It is imperative for schools to prioritize the deployment of professionally intelligent and well-trained officers to ensure the most suitable response to negative juvenile or criminal behavior.

Prospective officers enter the field of policing with a variety of motivations. Some are driven by a desire to protect, serve, and preserve lives, while others may be attracted to the esteem, prestige, and privileges associated with the profession.

Unfortunately, there are those who are drawn by the allure of power and authority that comes with the role. Often, those with malicious motivations are exposed after negative incidents occur. There are instances where problematic officers are reassigned to work as school police officers to mitigate the likelihood of future bad acts on the streets. Officers that have the inclination of arrests for statistical points over intervention can create an environment where students feel that any misstep will lead to a statistically added encounter with police. The practice further complicates the argument for having officers in schools.

Statistical-Based Policing

Law enforcement operates within a framework that is heavily reliant on data. Agencies base practices on statistical insights, using data to justify a variety of responses such as resource allocation. Statistical data can be used as performance motivators and increased arrest numbers can be interpreted as signs of robust and effective police activity. There is increased apprehension regarding the presence of police in schools. Concerns arise from the assumption that the introduction of police in an educational setting may result in statistical-based interactions that lead to arrests and contribute to disproportionate outcomes that may harm students.

Moreover, there is a perception that interactions between police and students in a school environment might mirror similar interactions between police and adults where street tactics are used in the student encounter. Since student arrests may be used as data points to support requests for additional school based law policing resources, many question the extreme propensity of officers using intermediate weapons or other use-of-force applications against students for relatively minor infractions. School policing leadership establishes the department's tone to ensure the best outcomes for students. The more effective approach of student advocacy and emphasizes alternatives to criminal justice involvement might conflict with anticipated outcomes tied to statistically driven policing strategies that prioritize arrests or citations.

Metrics such as increased arrest rates, drug confiscations, and traffic citations serve as statistical indicators and justifications for requests for increased funding. Basic interactions such as issuing citations for relatively minor infractions may provide statistical data points but also have the potential to hinder student progress, particularly when more effective alternatives exist but are neglected. Minor negative interactions may cause a student to interpret police responses as overreactions or as a fear-inducing strategy that leads to an escalated incident. The effectiveness of school police services should not be determined primarily by the number of juvenile arrests made.

Department initiatives that encourage student arrests to increase relevance through statistical data can inappropriately incentivize officers to prioritize arrests over advocacy. Tracking student arrest data is important for understanding the volume and nature of crimes occurring within a campus or district; however, arrest data should not be promoted as a measurement of officer effectiveness. A more beneficial student advocacy data point that should be measured in school policing is the number of students handled for criminal offenses that were successfully diverted from the criminal justice system through alternative diversionary solutions.

Law Enforcement/Educator Alignment

Critics argue that by maintaining a constant police presence in schools, the constitutional rights of many students may be in jeopardy. Increased student referrals to the police, irrespective of the nature of the infraction, are identified as indicators of concern. The fear that marginalized student groups are subjected to a disproportionate number of negative police interactions and police searches add to the argument against police in schools. Campus-based practices that have a heavy reliance on police intervention into situations that fall outside the typical scope of police duties only compound concerns.

The lines of demarcation between school police and campus administrator roles often blur. Specific responsibilities related to noncriminal offenses must remain clearly delineated between police and administrators to prevent the occurrence of inadvertent harm to student educational progress. This is not to suggest that negative student behavior should be disregarded. However, disciplinary actions that result in suspension or expulsion must be carefully considered due to the long-term impact on student success. Many states passed laws to expressly forbid school-based law enforcement officers from engaging in matters related to student discipline. Police and school administrator responses should be applied in a manner that holds students accountable while incorporating outcomes that provide protection and relief for a victim.

Additionally, solutions should include actions taken that promote student growth, learning, and progression of the offender that mitigates reoffending. The benefits of such practices create a layer to overall campus safety and security.

> Quick Tip: If you have school resource officers assigned to your school, whether full-time or as a shared resource across your district, set a time to sit down and get to know them like other employees or peers. Understanding their perspective, their experience, and their areas of focus can enable a much more effective and complimentary working relationship for your school. Set goals together and look for opportunities to support their career goals while benefiting your school or district.

Many options are available to enhance campus security. Although effective strategies to improve student safety and well-being exist, some strategies produce unintended consequences. Zero-tolerance policies in school districts aimed to reduce and deter crime and punish juvenile offenders is one such strategy. The perceived successes that result from increased student arrests for drug possession, assaults, and weapons offenses creates a sense of safety and inspires the expansion of police presence on campuses. However, according to Skiba, Arredondo, and Williams, zero-tolerance practices produce an increased number of student arrests and the overcriminalization of student behavior, particularly among marginalized student populations.[4] Furthermore, the criminalization of immature, emotional, mental, and adolescent behavior becomes pervasive, and the practice has potential to increase negative encounters between marginalized students and school police. The residual effects of such encounters can impact students into adulthood, creating lasting coping challenges related to real-world issues.

Overdependence on School-Based Police Services

Over the past two decades, a growing intersectionality between schools and the criminal justice system has emerged. School districts have an increased dependency on law enforcement intervention which includes the monitoring of noncriminal student activity in an effort to discourage potential criminal behavior. Critics argue that such a reliance has reached a point where some school campuses resemble quasi-prison communities. Zero-tolerance practices do not always eliminate disruptive or negative student behavior but consistently contribute to the increase in student suspensions, disciplinary actions, and arrests. According to Black, an overemphasis on forced compliance under zero-tolerance practices have led to student suspensions for acts as minor as chewing a pop tart into the shape of a gun.[5]

Arcia suggests that the use of suspension as a disciplinary measure has a detrimental impact on student academic achievement. Such actions can have a dramatic influence on student growth.[6]

Exposing students to the juvenile or criminal justice system, particularly during their formative years and beyond, can result in lasting adverse effects on their future involvement in the system. Moreover, there is a correlation between suspensions and expulsions and an elevated student dropout rate or delayed graduations. The argument that zero-tolerance policies increase positive school climates becomes more difficult to sustain, particularly when associated with negative achievement and gaps created in student outcomes.

Protocols developed to govern police engagement in response to violent or aggressive incidents in schools may resemble the zero-tolerance actions, practices, and policing tactics used by officers patrolling high crime areas in cities around the country. However, the fragmentation and inconsistencies in school policing practices create differences of expectations, tactics, mindsets, and strategies. While officers should have access to less-lethal weapon options, the use of tasers on students by school-based law enforcement results in intense scrutiny. Careful consideration should be given to approved use-of-force options deployed in a school environment. Restraint techniques like chokeholds on students raises significant concerns and is a highly prohibited use-of-force option. Negative police use-of-force outcomes in schools may call to question the quality, decision-making abilities, and training of officers hired to serve in an educational environment.

A variety of school policing strategies aimed at enhancing community and school safety have emerged in the United States. Several strategies have proven to be significant, while others have yielded unanticipated outcomes that exacerbated negative perceptions about police due to system failures in the alignment between educators and police.[7]

Despite the challenges, modern school-based police agencies remain undeterred in their efforts to implement innovative strategies designed to reverse negative trends in the postmodern era of school-based policing. Postmodern policing initiatives encompass a wide range of programs, strategies, and collaborative partnership initiatives.

Contracted School Police Services or School District Police Services

Districts have a variety of options when exploring the addition of police services. Options include hiring contracted school resource officers, establishing a school district police department, or, in certain states, utilizing school marshals or guardians. The role of citizen involvement such as volunteer campus security staff should not be overlooked. Law enforcement agencies acknowledge that collaboration with the community is an indispensable component in preserving the safety of students, staff, and school campuses.

The question is often raised regarding the benefits of having contracted police services through an SRO program or creating a district police department. School districts enter into contract police services for SROs and acquire the services of a variety of law enforcement agencies from municipal, county, or college police departments. SROs are licensed peace officers and are typically affiliated with a law enforcement agency that has overlapping jurisdiction where a school district is located. Depending on a school district's geographical boundaries, SROs from multiple agencies may be contracted to provide police services for a single district. There are benefits to selecting SROs to serve school districts, but there are existing challenges that must be considered.

School districts generally consider SRO programs as a cost-effective option that improves safety and security services without the added financial burden related to startup costs and the annual operation of a district police department. Utilizing SROs relieves school districts of mandatory state requirements for operating an independent law enforcement agency. However, the tradeoff is that school districts relinquish control over the quality, type, or training level of the officers provided, as SROs typically follow the training guidelines of the law enforcement agency of hire. Through contract service agreements, a law enforcement entity provides police services to a school district. Officers selected for the SRO program are trained to respond to on campus critical incidents and criminal activity, which reduces response times during emergencies. Unlike school district police officers, SROs are not employees of a school district; instead, they operate under a contractual agreement and school district partnership.

Law enforcement objectives can vary between agencies since each has distinct parameters and operational objectives based upon the organizational leadership and jurisdiction served. Each agency has differing leadership styles and unique department specific policies and expectations. Officers are required to meet and uphold the training standards set by their respective law enforcement agency. Variations between law enforcement agencies and the services provided can produce inconsistencies in the quality, availability, and approach to school policing.

SROs are typically assigned to different campuses, including middle, elementary, and high schools, or disciplinary alternative education centers. Expectations, duties, and responsibilities of SROs may vary based on the mission and vision of the law enforcement agency providing the police services. The priority of SROs is first to their law enforcement agency of hire, followed by the needs and expectations of the contracted school district. In situations involving critical incidents off-campus that require an immediate police response, SROs may be obligated to respond despite creating a coverage gap on the school campus.

SRO training is coordinated based on the needs of the law enforcement agency of hire rather than the overall needs of the school district. Conflicting priorities can occur when off-site SRO training is scheduled during a regular school day and the SRO is mandated to attend. In the absence of a trained SRO, unskilled or untrained replacement officers may be assigned to cover campuses. The temporarily assigned officer may lack a familiarity of the campus layout and safety protocols. Furthermore, the officer may lack established relationships or connections with students and staff, which are crucial to initiating and maintaining positive engagement.

> Quick Tip: In addition to meeting with your SRO, set up a meeting with department leadership from the SRO's agency. This can range from the chief in a small department, to a lieutenant, or sergeant in a larger agency. Use this meeting to specifically discuss known points of friction and begin to develop a more cohesive relationship to minimize friction and maximize collaborative work.

In the United States, school districts employ policing services through a variety of approaches. While many schools opt for SRO services, others establish their own school district police departments. There are unique advantages to having a school district police department dedicated to providing specialized law enforcement services to a school district. School district police departments bring an unparalleled level of stability and consistency. It allows a school district more control over officer selection, training standards, department vision, and specific policing methods. Officers serve as a constant presence capable of fostering strong and enduring relationships with students, staff, and parents.

The opportunity and capacity exists to dismantle historical barriers that have impeded genuine collaboration between school district administrators and the police. School district police officers as employees, are in a unique position to prioritize a district specific and coordinated safety needs. This can include specialized active shooter, threat mitigation, and campus crime deterrence initiatives in coordination with campus administrators and staff. SROs are encouraged, but generally not required to train or align with campus administrator directives.

Additionally, department policies and training strategies for SROs may not always align with school district philosophies regarding student advocacy and law enforcement intervention.

School district police departments offer a higher level of efficiency in rapid response. Officers are well-acquainted with specific campus safety protocols and campus layouts. Furthermore, officers train alongside school staff to ensure an efficient response to critical incidents. Establishing relationships with parents provides district police officers with more opportunities for student advocacy and enables greater parental involvement in the effective resolution of student-related concerns. However, there are trade-offs to the inherent advantages of starting a school district police department. This might include financial constraints associated with the initial startup and annual operating costs and the transfer of civil liability for officer actions or inactions.

Critics of school policing recognize that prioritizing school safety is essential but express concerns regarding the potentially negative impact of deploying additional officers in a school environment. Districts with their own police departments can formulate strategies to shift district reliance from a heavy reliance on law enforcement intervention for noncriminal and minor student infractions. Officers have the opportunity to engage in mentorship, student advocacy, and relationship-building. The option provides a mechanism for the development of holistic student care while optimizing long-term and beneficial student outcomes.

Social Workers in School-Based Police Departments

Behavioral health resources are vital to ensuring the continued development of students, especially when incorporating social workers into a school district police department. Behavioral health professionals provide intervention during crises that may arise from social, emotional, behavioral, substance abuse, or mental health needs of students. Social workers provide case management and comprehensive support services to families, ensuring they have appropriate resources conducive to beneficial student outcomes. Moreover, social workers collaborate with officers and provide alternative solutions for proper intervention. Incidents occur on campuses where school staff and police may have perceived a student's actions as noncompliance. In reality, the behavior was actually a manifestation of a social, emotional, behavioral, substance abuse, or mental health issue. A failure to distinguish between manifested behavioral health acts with underlying issues can contribute to increased student referrals to law enforcement.

The stages of adolescent development often manifest a limited comprehension of the long-term implications, repercussions, and outcomes of their actions. Juvenile and adolescent minds, being highly susceptible to influence, underscore the significance of law enforcement interaction as an opportunity to have a positive or negative impact on their lives. Adverse, impulsive, and reckless juvenile behavior may stem from immaturity, but can also be an indicator of underlying behavioral, social, and emotional issues. It is crucial for officers and school staff to be well trained in the recognition of key indicators that unveil the root causes and motivations behind student misbehavior. Moreover, school district police officers and school staff must be prepared to address behavioral concerns adeptly, understanding the "why" behind negative juvenile behavior, in order to develop effective solutions for addressing underlying contributing factors that trigger crises.

> Quick Tip: School security personnel, SROs, and school and district leadership should meet to set coordinated priorities and protocols and establish expectations for communication and information-sharing. The relationship between school security staff and the SRO/law enforcement should be as seamless as possible, and this requires proactive work to ensure effective communications are maintained throughout the school year.

In 2020, the Round Rock ISD Police Department was the first known school district in the United States to implement a solution that included the addition of fifteen social workers to the school district police department.[8]

While the concept of social workers and school police officers operating within the same department is relatively novel in the United States, it has been implemented in several traditional law enforcement agencies for many years.

The initiative was designed to bring licensed master social workers and licensed clinical social workers to the department so that student crisis situations related to social, emotional, behavioral, mental, or substance abuse could be handled effectively without law enforcement intervention. Some student crisis situations can mimic criminality, and the manifestations are beyond the ability of a student to control. Having experts trained to distinguish between the two was beneficial in ensuring that students received ongoing support and wrap-around services were provided for families to ensure beneficial student outcomes.

In many schools, interaction between police officers and social workers is minimal and can result in a divergence of perspectives, goals, and strategies. Operating independently can hinder the added value of the partnership. Successful joint efforts are challenged by the lack of a true cultural shift, clearly established expectations, and a unified approach in service delivery. Social workers generally focus on identifying root causes and contributing factors, aiming to provide resources and support to students and families during crises. Conversely, criminal justice system intervention, which is not typically a primary consideration for social workers, is often the "go-to" response for law enforcement officers in dealing with criminal offenses. A crucial factor for successful collaboration is the proper alignment and integration of expectations and outcomes between social workers and police officers. This alignment ensures that both disciplines work cohesively toward common goals, enhancing the overall effectiveness of their joint efforts in educational settings.

When combining social workers and police officers, it is crucial to enhance their mutual understanding and perspectives while ensuring that the objectives of their services are aligned. Police officers, with their extensive training in law enforcement, safety, and criminal justice, complement the expertise of social workers, who are proficient in handling emotional distress and problematic behaviors. Social workers have the training to more accurately identify concealed or underlying issues in students. By uniting these distinct skill sets within a single department, a comprehensive approach to school policing is formed. This integration leads to a more efficient and effective way of supporting student outcomes, leveraging the combined strengths of both professions. The collaboration promotes daily interaction and mutual understanding of the roles each discipline has, while fostering students' long-term success and a positive school atmosphere. Success not only requires the merging of the two subject matter areas but also the right leadership and the proper selection process for hiring social workers and officers in the pursuit of student safety and security at the highest levels.

School-Based Police Officer Selection

The process of selecting officers to serve in schools is a critical step and must be performed with fidelity to ensure that students are properly served by officers who possess the appropriate temperament, mindset, and skill sets suitable for a school environment. Although many officers possess the necessary skills to adapt training and tactics to the school environment, some may struggle with the adjustment to dealing with adolescent behavior and actions that can mimic adult actions, behaviors, and aggressions.

Schools with campus police typically utilize officers for a variety of support services, including monitoring student activities, patrolling school grounds, and maintaining a peaceful and secure academic environment. Tragic occurrences like school shootings at Columbine High School, Sandy Hook Elementary, Marjory Stoneman Douglas High School, Santa Fe High School, and Robb Elementary School prompted legislators around the country to reallocate resources specific to implementing effective measures designed to prevent future tragedies. Tragic school violence incidents highlight emerging opportunities to improve safety through innovative and effective strategies. Comprehensive assessments of school safety and policing practices, both before and after critical incidents, remain imperative to implementing appropriate measures to mitigate the likelihood of future occurrences.

The duties of school-based police officers encompass much more than responding to active shooters, making arrests, or intervening in criminal situations. The law enforcement profession is in a perpetual state of improvement. Historical approaches to policing were seemingly pragmatic with strategies crafted to achieve specific outcomes. Consequently, aspects of outdated practices persist today. School-based policing demands a unique skill set that fosters beneficial outcomes for students. Officers are a critical component to effective school safety but also serve as valuable resources in areas such as student advocacy, equity, and behavioral health. School-based policing is a specialized area of law enforcement. Officers engage daily in mentoring, advocacy, encouragement, and address challenges in ways that eliminate historical barriers. The depth and impact of officer involvement has the potential to dramatically increase student success.

The Art of School-Based Policing

Although arguments exist to suggest that police in schools are an avenue for students entering the criminal justice system at a higher rate, counterarguments suggest that the presence of police decreases crime.[9]

The inherent deterrent component of having the proper police present on campuses lowers the likelihood of negative or criminal behavior that might otherwise occur in the absence of officers. Policing is an art, and the substance of the profession must remain malleable in the hands of those who work to perfect the craft. It demands imagination, innovation, and information. The art of policing should be in a perpetual state of evolution mixed with new ideas that flow from the experiences and unique opportunities to positively influence perspectives and lives.

> Quick Tip: The establishment of a robust and multidisciplinary threat assessment team that is well-trained and operates through a clearly and objectively defined process is critical to supporting school safety. Embrace the threat assessment process and the communication opportunities and challenges presented by this multidisciplinary team, and seek opportunities to support additional training and resources to this team.

The foundational role of police officers is that of a "peace" officer, as defined by statutes in numerous states across the nation. The term "peace officer" embodies the countless altruistic deeds performed each day by men and women called to serve in the law enforcement profession. Officers understand that thousands of positive actions and lifesaving acts performed by dedicated professionals can be overshadowed by the misdeeds of a single individual in uniform. Nevertheless, policing should remain an art of perpetual evolution that allows the canvas to contain the fingerprints of empathetic policing practices, respectful interactions, and true relationship building in all communities.

The art of policing can be an inferior product when viewed from the works of officers lacking in training, temperament, or discipline that is needed for success in an educational environment. For this reason, a deliberate devotion to the art must be made to develop the skills to improve the product produced. School-based policing is an ever-evolving process that is most effective when meeting the needs of society is prioritized. Effective practices can rehabilitate negative perceptions that students may hold about police. When applied properly, the art of school policing can become a masterpiece that allows students to see beyond the uniform. It reveals a person behind the badge with a mindset dedicated to student advocacy and a commitment to protecting and serving the best interests of all students.

Some schools recognize the unique contributions that school-based police officers can provide and use them to teach career and technology education courses in criminal justice. Students participating in classroom instruction tend to exhibit more positive attitudes toward officers. Beger and Hartnett contend that regular student interactions with school-based police officers has a beneficial impact on shaping attitudes and feelings of many students.[10]

The more interaction students have with school-based police officers, the more positive the attitudes and perceptions become toward officers. Additionally, interactions can increase positive attitudes from officers' perspectives toward students in a way that corrects misperceptions. As interactions increase, the attitudes and beliefs about officer fairness and competence can also increase. However, students with limited interactions throughout the school year experience the smallest impact on their sense of school connectedness.

A crucial component to the success of a school district police department is community engagement. It is a beneficial partnership that school district police departments can cultivate at a more impactful level to create awareness, transparency, and support. Conducting regular meetings with stakeholders, including those with apprehensions about school police, provides platforms for meaningful discussions and solutions.

Although criminal behavior is generally not prevalent in elementary schools and tends to be more common at the middle and high school levels, campus safety priorities exist for all. The presumption should not be made that assigning police officers is unnecessary due to the low number of police-related incidents. Concerns at the elementary school level should not be minimized, particularly since two of the most tragic school shootings in the United States happened at Sandy Hook Elementary in Newton, Connecticut, in 2012, and Robb Elementary School in Uvalde, Texas, in 2022. The presence of police on elementary school campuses provides an effective deterrent and quick response solution to potential criminal activity. Police officers at elementary schools are generally perceived by students as superheroes, and negative interactions are relatively low. Furthermore, the scarcity of criminal offenses and the age range of criminal responsibility prevent criminal justice intervention in most instances. School districts must ensure that officers assigned to campuses are trained to respond appropriately to a variety of situations regardless of student ages or campus type.

School-Based Policing Training Gaps and Opportunities

Police academies across the United States graduate thousands of cadets annually. Although school districts commonly contract with local law enforcement agencies for police services, academies often lack specialized training modules tailored to school policing. Consequently, school districts are compelled to hire officers trained to navigate dynamic and high-stress situations in environments other than a school setting. The absence of a dedicated school police training academy limits options for school districts and places a significant portion of training reliance on training received on the job.

Police academy training emphasizes a variety of learning objectives, including traffic laws, criminal offenses, drug offenses, officer survival, and weapons training. Officers graduate from police academies with a basic understanding of juvenile laws related to delinquent conduct and proper law enforcement response to children in need of supervision or CINS. According to the U.S. Census Bureau, the population in the United States between the ages of ten and eighteen is approximately forty-one million as of 2020.[11]

However, juvenile law or police/juvenile encounter training is often relegated to on-the-job learning which varies greatly throughout the country. Advocacy training related to juvenile rights is not a priority, and little academic exploration is given to the long-term consequences of juvenile incarceration. Officers who transition from street policing to school-based policing may inadvertently apply policing methods and tactics designed for areas and situations outside of school.

> Quick Tip: Integrating School Police Officers and specifically School Resource Officers into the campus leadership and both staff and student culture is a critical component to the success of the program. Simple visual cues such as adding the school mascot to the graphics on a police cruiser reinforce that concept. Great concepts to discuss with your SRO.

Despite potential misperceptions surrounding the qualifications of school-based law enforcement officers, licensing requirements remain consistent with those for any other state-certified peace officer. School-based law enforcement undergo the same training at state-approved police academies and adhere to mandated training requirements that meet minimum state requirements for police officer certification. As school policing evolves, the role of school-based law enforcement officers is increasingly being recognized as an area of specialization. An emerging perspective within law enforcement acknowledges that most juvenile criminal behavior stems from immaturity or a manifestation of deeper social, emotional, or mental challenges, which cannot be adequately resolved through the implementation of criminal justice strategies. In response, school-based policing increasingly utilizes contemporary policing strategies that focus on intervention and diversionary solutions as preferred options for handling delinquent juvenile behavior.

Historically, law enforcement's approach to handling juvenile delinquency prioritized a spontaneous and retributive response to negative behavior. The primary objective and expectation required officers to remedy the existing child related issue and return to what they considered to be "real police work." However, this approach inadvertently raised the probability of repeat juvenile offenders facing increased criminal charges for minor acts to bring swift justice, discourage future wrongdoing, and to send a message to other juveniles of the expected outcomes if similar actions were committed. This approach contributed to the overcriminalization of juvenile behavior and the disproportionate representation of school-aged juveniles in the court system.[12]

Training officers to identify cues and behaviors that necessitate specific interventions, such as involving social workers, counselors, or other support staff in situations as alternatives to police intervention is a valuable skill. Students can benefit from practices that detach officers from involvement in disciplinary procedures. This approach can significantly reduce adverse police interactions in noncriminal situations. By fostering environments rich in student advocacy and by emphasizing the utilization of resources other than the criminal justice system to address student conduct, fair and beneficial outcomes for students can be improved.

> Quick Tip: There is an extensive array of training that is specifically designed for today's school resource officer. As a school or district, consider funding the $50 annual membership for your SRO to the National Association of School Resource Officers, which includes a multitude of resources and discounted high-quality training for SROs.

School district police departments have the latitude to establish specific training criteria and other initiatives centered on overall student well-being. Officers are able to identify alternative pathways and utilize diverse resources to divert students from the criminal justice system, particularly for minor infractions. Specialized training in these areas can create an organizational environment that recognizes the cultural values of all individuals while promoting fair treatment and equal opportunities for success. Incorporating training modules in restorative practices, mental health first aid, Trust-Based Relational Intervention (TBRI), de-escalation techniques, threat mitigation, and active shooter response prepares officers to effectively navigate a variety of scenarios within an educational institution. Inadequate training in these areas can create disparate outcomes for some student groups. Lack of training can cause disrespectful, immature, and adolescent behavior to be viewed as criminal acts. Creating a department grounded in transformative and student-centric policing approaches generates positive results that can alter perceptions and increase support for the inclusion of law enforcement in educational environments.

> Quick Tip: When opportunities for security-related training present themselves, whether locally hosted or national training conferences, consider expanding beyond safety and security personnel to other members of your staff as your resources allow. This deepens your resource pool, provides a spectrum of perspectives, and maximizes support across your entire staff. This is also key to developing a sense of responsibility in every employee for their role in keeping the school safe and secure.

Police officers undergo extensive training across various specialized areas and within specific disciplines. Detectives assigned to investigating cases related to crimes committed against children receive training in the specific discipline that is not provided to patrol officers. The relevance of the training to the specific environment or specialization served is crucial, as officers are entrusted with maintaining a high level of expertise and academic vigilance to improve the performance of their duties. It is imperative for officers to respond thoughtfully to student behavior and for actions to be based on articulable facts that have a direct and legal law enforcement nexus. Failure to do so may lead to inappropriate police responses that lead to unfavorable encounters for affected students.

For instance, the mischaracterization or unwarranted "labeling" of students solely on the types of music they listen to or fashion choices could raise unjustifiable suspicions, false assumptions, or inquisitive inquiry by police compared to the suspicions or assumptions raised about students who express a strong interest in classical music or mathematics. School-based law enforcement officers have a responsibility to consistently assess and calibrate policing practices to ensure consistency and alignment with the environment served. The ongoing evaluation and calibration of practices will ensure that policing strategies align with expected practices that consistently yield positive outcomes for students.

Inexperienced and untrained officers may find it more difficult to properly interpret actual student actions, motivations, and needs. The process to develop the level of sensitivity needed to respond effectively to existing challenges takes time and deliberate alignment. Although crimes committed by students have decreased over the past decade, student suspensions and expulsions have increased with Black students at a rate approximately three times higher than white students.[13]

Regardless of the background or life experiences of a student, each deserves to be protected from the ill effects of social and environmental influences that are onramps to the criminal justice system. Officers trained to identify the various challenges that students face and the resulting manifestations may be more effective at addressing specific needs through resources designed to reduce the impulses that lead to negative behavior. Properly trained police officers have the capability to serve as advocates and beacons of hope to remove barriers and guide students toward opportunities of success.

Student Internal Pain and Frustrations Experienced vs. Visibly Manifested

Effective school police officers must recognize the reality of hidden contributing factors. A variety of external actions and behaviors can trigger regressed trauma that a student actively tries to suppress. Officers that embrace the art of policing understand that traumatic student experiences can lead to post-traumatic stress disorder (PTSD). Rather than quickly exposing concealed wounds, the objective should be to respond in a manner that promotes healing. Situations where a student is negatively impacted by a police officer's actions or reactions can hinder trust, security, and recovery.

Recognizing triggers requires a delicate approach to ensure that accurate conclusions are reached so that the most effective support and resources can be allocated, and the proper resolution achieved. If approached with a sincerity of practice and commitment, the art of school policing becomes a beautiful masterpiece that can be appreciated by the practitioners, recipients, and observers. It is crucial for officers to acquire the skills needed for effective school policing. Officers can become career practitioners, deeply immersed in the art, and serve as examples for others in the profession. Practitioners of the art must learn the proper application, while leaders in the profession should continuously evaluate strategies to ensure that practices are specifically tailored to the needs of the students and districts served.

The importance of ensuring the proper and specialized training of school-based police officers cannot be overstated. The catalyst for change begins at the top with executive leadership of law enforcement agencies that provide police services. Although mandated training for school-based police officers exists, there is a lack of training specific to leadership of school-based policing providers. Consequently, tactics and procedures programmed into line level officers may carry over from the training they received from community-based policing to their assignments in school districts. Tactics such as those that promote zero-tolerance practices limit student growth, development, and overall success. Additionally, it dramatically hinders educator intervention and advocacy opportunities when students commit minor criminal offenses.

Training Needs for School-Based Police Executive Leadership

Emphasis is needed on mandatory training for executive leadership that provide school police services. An effective leadership training solution would ensure that executives establish initiatives to increase the level of understanding among school-based police officers related to cognitive and behavioral differences between the handling of youth and adults. The

> **University of Nevada, Las Vegas (UNLV), Las Vegas, Nevada**
>
> On December 6, 2023, at approximately 11:45 a.m., an identified male shooter, 67, armed with a handgun, began shooting people at UNLV in Las Vegas, Nevada. Three people (employees) were killed; one person (a visiting professor) was wounded. The shooter was killed by law enforcement at the scene following an exchange of gunfire.
>
> www.fbi.gov

Figure 2.2. University of Nevada, Las Vegas. www.fbi.gov

approach would help to emphasize the need for advocacy based policing in school environments. Police practices utilized and that may be considered acceptable when dealing with adults in communities may be incongruent with acceptable practices required in a school environment.

Actions and tactics used by police officers should be dictated by the environment or arena of service. The practice and art of school policing requires law enforcement executives to develop effective strategies that align stakeholders and establish shared objectives that best serve all students. Aligning police objectives with school district and community expectations can be a challenge. Effective methods to create alignment should include identifying key goals designed to enhance the quality of service provided for students, gathering input regarding desired goals, and clear expectations from school staff and community members. Once data is compiled, a comparative analysis should be conducted to identify shared goals, assess alignment efficiencies, and prioritize critical objectives that can enhance student outcomes.

Psychological Assessments for School-Based Policing

The process of selecting officers for school policing roles should be rigorous and highly selective. Requirements should be consistent with advanced level guidelines and criteria used to select officers entering specialized areas within the law enforcement profession and beyond entry-level patrol positions. Selection processes should include psychological examinations to evaluate a potential candidate's ability to serve in a school environment. A variety of screening examinations such as the Minnesota Multiphasic Personality Inventory (MMPI) are used to identify predictors of potentially problematic behaviors in new police candidates.[14]

State commissions on law enforcement require new police candidates to take psychological examinations upon entering the profession. Upon passing the entry-level examination, many officers can complete an entire career without being required to submit to another psychological examination.

Officers can receive numerous promotions and be exposed to countless traumatic events without a state mandated screening requirement. A sound best practice is to require psychological assessments for potential school police officer candidates prior to serving in the field of school-based policing. The Round Rock ISD Police Department in Round Rock, Texas, implemented a mandatory psychological screening requirement for all officers. An examination was conducted every five years or after a traumatic event such as an officer's direct involvement in a shooting incident. The purpose was to ensure that any psychological issues that officers faced were identified and the proper support and resources were allocated to ensure their overall well-being.

Specific criteria should be measured through pre-employment psychological examinations that include temperament, mindset, and adaptability inventories. Although temperament can be influenced by both innate personality traits and environmental factors, assessing aspects of a candidate's temperament, it can reveal a tendency toward aggression, patience, empathy, and impulse control. Standardized tests and questionnaires are often used to evaluate these traits. Assessing a candidate's mindset, particularly in terms of attitudes toward aligning the goals of leadership, individual responsibility, and ethical behavior, can help to determine the synergistic potential of an individual.

Personal views on use of force, bias awareness, the ability to handle stress, and ethical decision-making skills can be examined. Adaptability is essential in law enforcement and can reveal a level of perspective through psychological testing. Adaptability includes identifying a candidate's coping ability and response to change effectiveness. It can provide a glimpse of how a candidate responds effectively to change, handles complex situations, and thinks creatively. Scenarios and situational judgment tests might be used to assess this component. Human behavior is complex and influenced by a wide range of factors. While psychological exams can provide key insight, examinations do not predict future behavior or performance.

Factors such as temperament, disciplinary history, psychological well-being, mindset, adaptability, and personal motivation are critical factors to consider when selecting officers to work in a school environment. Officers seeking to work in a school should demonstrate a genuine desire to serve students in an educational environment. The motivation should not be based solely on incentives that come with the position such as day shifts or weekends off.

Leaders should select officers with a genuine interest in assisting students, removing obstacles, and fulfilling a calling to student advocacy. It should include selecting officers who can break down barriers that hinder students from reaching their fullest potential. Officers must prioritize service to students over themselves. A commitment to service above personal gain is essential. Earning respect is more valuable than earning a paycheck. Emphasizing the importance of establishing relationships founded on trust and mutual respect can foster a productive educational setting. It is imperative for law enforcement leaders to integrate a continuous cultural understanding into the genuine practices and approaches of officers assigned to school-based law enforcement roles.

> Quick Tip: Depending on the size of the agency that your SRO is part of, they may have the opportunity (or requirement) to fill in or be regularly scheduled for standard patrol shifts. Although typically seen as a detriment by schools, these opportunities are very important for the SRO to maintain their patrol skills and integrate with their agency peers. These opportunities reinforce critical officer survival skills and ensure that the SRO remains well-connected with their parent agency.

The mindset of school-based police officers must remain rooted in the understanding that students are in various phases of cognitive development where the long-term consequences of their actions are not fully comprehended. Hiring officers with a service-oriented mindset and exhibiting a strong commitment to place the needs of students as a priority can influence a dramatic culture shift. School-based policing leadership plays a pivotal role in achieving equitable partnerships with stakeholders that focus on transformative practices to support all students, including the most vulnerable. To be effective, leaders must be open to varying perspectives while minimizing power struggles and conflicts in pursuit of unified student advocacy. Collaboration through innovative policing can lead to the genuine integration of services and positively impact students and their families.

The significance of school-based law policing leadership extends beyond school-based policing. Presenting valuable training opportunities for executives across various law enforcement sectors can improve the quality of service provided by all officers. Leaders have the privilege to foster a shift from a strict "letter of the law" approach when policing juveniles to a more empathetic "spirit of the law" practice. The strategy not only promotes growth and development within law enforcement but also extends support to adults, offering alternatives in lieu of the criminal justice system.

As practitioners in law enforcement, police officers must remain in a continuous state of growth and development. Mastery of the role extends beyond the basic knowledge received in on-the-job training. It should be comprehensive in areas of juvenile justice, de-escalation practices, conflict resolution, and restorative practices. Challenges arise when officers presume mastery without a full understanding of the elements required for success. School-based policing requires intentionality to develop the ability to eliminate existing weaknesses to achieve a level of efficiency needed to serve students and the community.

Reducing Law Enforcement Involvement in Minor Incidents

In Texas, Senate Bill 393 and SB1114 were enacted in 2015 to decrease the issuance of misdemeanor citations by police to students for minor offenses. The catalyst for the bills resulted from numerous instances where police issued students citations for a variety of seemingly minor offenses such as disruption of class for wearing excessive perfume. Instances when a student was arrested for theft after taking a low-cost chicken nugget meal from school, valued at less than three dollars, highlighted the need for dramatic change.

Senate Bill 393 dealt with criminal procedures related to citations, penalties, and prosecution for certain minor offenses committed by students. It prohibited Texas school district police officers from issuing citations to students for Class C misdemeanors involving disruptions in class or on school buses. Instead, officers seeking to charge students with certain minor offenses are required to file a formal complaint with a judge instead of issuing a citation.

Except for traffic offenses or public intoxication, Senate Bill 1114 prohibits law enforcement officers from issuing citations to students under the age of twelve for behavior occurring at school or on school transportation. Additionally, it disallowed arrest warrants for students who violated minor criminal offenses found in the Texas Education Code. The legislative response sought to reduce the excessive overreaction to adolescent behavior and prevented situations where students faced disciplinary action for behaviors that would not have historically been considered alarming or disruptive.

Despite changes in state laws, disproportionate disciplinary practices heighten the likelihood that marginalized student groups will enter the criminal justice system at high rates. Consequently, students often encounter school police referrals or face expulsion due to procedures intended to eliminate disruptive students from school premises, ostensibly to preserve control and safety. The intense pressure on school districts to enhance academic performance may inadvertently justify heightened punitive measures and disciplinary actions. The removal of disruptive students appears rooted in the assumption that it effectively sustains a peaceful and conducive learning atmosphere. However, the practice is not equitable and can potentially negatively impact students by denying them access to the educational services that they need. Achieving equitable outcomes is important to ensuring that the needs of all students are met.

Equity in education is about identifying and meeting the needs of all students to empower and transfer the ownership of success to the individual student. Students in crisis may manifest an underlying issue in a variety of ways, including disruptive outburst, noncompliance, and aggressive behavior. Removing a student who manifests disruptive behaviors is considered an effective approach for restoring peace and maintaining a safe learning environment. Removing a student and placing them in detention or in school suspension may be beneficial to a segment of the school environment but the response may not resolve underlying issues the student that caused the disruption might be struggling to overcome. The problem is compounded when police are parties in the removal process when no law enforcement nexus exists. Some students struggle with underlying issues that can be triggered by a variety of internal and external influences.

Officers must approach every student with empathy, sympathy, and compassion, in pursuit of determining the best solutions apart from criminal justice options to meet student needs.

Adapting to a school environment requires officers to be receptive and open to change, particularly in areas where traditional policing practices may be incompatible with the needs and expectations within a controlled educational environment. Implementing effective change requires deliberate effort. Uncompromising presumptive ideas and beliefs tend to hinder the assimilation of new knowledge, information, and concepts. Through effective conceptual change practices, school-based law enforcement officers can foster positive transformation. It can motivate and inspire individuals to embrace new ideas and discard misconceptions that lead to negative experiences based upon flawed ideologies.

Students bring preexisting perceptions of police into an educational environment and preconceived notions heavily influence the level of desire to interact with officers. Students with negative past experiences or arrests may be less inclined to report crimes or incidents of victimization if perceptions of police are negative. Recognizing existing gaps between students and campus police officers provides an opportunity for collaboration, built on mutual respect and a continuous effort to build bridges of understanding that foster a safe and positive culture.

Historically, the primary response to negative student behavior in schools was to contact parents or guardians to address issues. If a student was involved in an altercation at school, parents, guardians, or family members responded to effectively address the incident. Today, a prevailing trend is that schools rely on disciplinary measures that may not always align with actions that parents or guardians consider to be in the best interest of the student. Moreover, communication with parents or guardians may be delayed or occurs after an investigation into the incident has concluded. Effective advocacy for students requires strong partnerships that involve parents and guardians. The immediate involvement of parents or guardians allows a student to have instant advocacy on their behalf to work toward a resolution that benefits all parties involved.

Officers and school staff can gain a greater level of understanding of student needs and challenges through actively listening to existing concerns. Listening to understand rather than listening for an opportunity to respond allows those in distress to express specific needs and concerns. Listening requires patience and understanding. It is predicated on building cohesion with students. Student advocacy is the art of determining what is needed and what effective strategies can be utilized to meet student needs. This approach allows for continual support and follow-up designed to gauge the impact of the services provided to ensure student well-being.

Students can be reluctant to confide in adults, particularly police officers. However, building relationships and prioritizing effective communication through active listening can unlock the full effects of student advocacy. Students need the latitude to learn from life mistakes and errors without facing lifelong penalties such as a permanent criminal record.

Student Advocacy Initiatives

Prioritizing student advocacy is vital to student success. Effective school-based police officers are those who are trained to take deliberate steps toward advocating for students. While informal, making student advocacy a priority for both law enforcement and school districts can yield significant long-term student benefits. The return on the investment can be seen in the removal of historical barriers that once impeded student success. In addition, it reduces the reliance on police intervention and the criminal justice system as primary resolution options.

Effective student advocacy involves moving away from a reliance on the criminal justice system to address negative behavior. Collaborating with departments within the juvenile justice system allows for alternative solutions and resources to be identified and maximized to support students through the most challenging situations. Officers can be trained to recognize potential underlying issues such as self-medication, social, or emotional issues found with drug use as a means of escape. In cases of minor drug offenses or possession, officers can rely on more effective alternatives to aid a student in overcoming addiction or other challenges they may face.

Additional services and resources can be provided to the family to help build their support capacity. Prioritizing student advocacy establishes a safer school environment and fosters better student outcomes. The objective is not to criminalize behaviors exhibited by students, like social, emotional, behavioral, or mental struggles, as the practice could significantly impact future growth. Criminalizing such behaviors can potentially increase the likelihood of reoffending.

> Quick Tip: Police officers come from a full spectrum of backgrounds. Law enforcement can often be a second career for many police officers. Previously credentialed teachers make great SROs, as do police officers who are looking to transition into teaching eventually as a next career opportunity. Educational incentives for SROs can be a shared benefit provided by the parent agency and the school district together.

The concept of school policing requires an emphasis on advocacy over arrests. Not all students feel a sense of true safety and protection in a school environment. Students classified as compliant, academically successful, or influential often feel more secure than students who might not fit those classifications. Critics argue that a diminished level of support, protection, and service often exists for students who do not fit the definition of a "good student." The art of school policing requires officers to recognize the capabilities and limitations of students and to utilize practices that enhance the development of identifiable, attainable, and sustainable solutions tailored to meet student needs. School-based policing should be approached as a thoughtful and intentional endeavor, delivering services to meet a variety of needs in the most equitable and constructive manner. Situations and student needs vary but the services provided by officers must remain student-centered and oriented toward achieving the best long-term outcomes. School policing practices must be implemented in a manner that creates an environment where students are confident enough to interact with police officers and not feel as if all actions or reactions are viewed with the ire of suspicion.

The practice must extend beyond the narrow focus on inquiry, investigation, and incarceration. Student interaction should be viewed from an advocacy lens, regardless of the circumstances. For example, dealing with highly disruptive students can trigger a need to shift priorities to a quick and peaceful resolution that may require an escalated police response. It is imperative that officers remain focused on the fundamental objective of student advocacy at all levels. Forcefully removing or arresting a student may provide rapid relief and resolution and restore peace in a learning environment. However, there should be efforts taken to help restore the peace within the disruptive student by seeking to identify and address the underlying issues that contributed to the disruption. The art of school policing demands that officers and school leaders consider diverse perspectives, allowing for the evaluation of various solutions, with the implementation of the most effective practices to ensure peaceful and impactful resolution and lasting student well-being.

Notes

1. Amanda Merkwae, "Schooling the Police: Race, Disability, and the Conduct of School Resource Officers," *Michigan Journal of Race & Law*, 21 (2015): 147–58.
2. United States Census Bureau, "Age and Sex Composition in the United States: 2020," accessed January 15, 2021. https://www.census.gov/data/tables/2020/demo/age-and-sex/2020-age-sex-composition.html.
3. Texas Commission on Law Enforcement. 2023. https://www.tcole.texas.gov/.
4. R. J. Skiba et al., "More than a Metaphor: The Contribution of Exclusionary Discipline to a School-to-Prison Pipeline," *Equity & Excellence in Education*, 47, no. 4 (2014): 546–64.
5. Derek W. Black, *Ending Zero Tolerance: The Crisis of Absolute School Discipline* (New York University Press, 2016).
6. Emily Arcia, "Achievement and Enrollment Status of Suspended Students: Outcomes in a Large, Multicultural School District," *Education and Urban Society*, 38, no. 3 (2006): 359–69.
7. Patricia Burch, *System Failure: Policy and Practice in the School-to-Prison Pipeline*, 1st ed. (Taylor and Francis, 2022).
8. Jeffrey D. Yarbrough, *Redefining School Safety and Policing: A Transformative Four Pillar Model* (Routledge, 2023).
9. Matthew T. Theriot, "An Empirical Analysis of School Resource Officer Interactions with Students," *Journal of Criminal Justice*, 37, no. 3 (2009): 280–7, https://doi.org:10.1016/j.jcrimjus.
10. Robert R. Bege and Susan M. Hartnett, "The Effects of Police Contact in Schools: An Examination of the Impact of Perceived Outcomes and Processes on Students," *Journal of Criminal Justice*, 46 (2016): 55–65. https://doi.org/10.1016/j.jcrimjus.2016.03.008.
11. United States Census Bureau, "Age and Sex Composition in the United States: 2020."
12. "The Overcriminalization of Youth in Our Public School Systems," *Juvenile Justice Update*, 21, no. 4 (2015): 3.
13. Kcyronne Q. Zahir, "School Suspension Rates Among Minority Males and Leadership Styles of Principals: Analysis of the Relationship as Measured by Discipline Consequences" (ProQuest Dissertations Publishing, 2023).

14. Anthony M. Tarescavage et al., "Minnesota Multiphasic Personality Inventory-2-Restructured Form (MMPI-2-RF) Predictors of Police Officer Problem Behavior and Collateral Self-Report Test Scores," *Psychological Assessment*, 27, no. 1 (2015): 125–37.

Bibliography

Arcia, Emily. "Achievement and Enrollment Status of Suspended Students: Outcomes in a Large, Multicultural School District." *Education and Urban Society*, 38, no. 3 (2006): 359–69.

Beger, Robert R., and Susan M. Hartnett. "The Effects of Police Contact in Schools: An Examination of the Impact of Perceived Outcomes and Processes on Students." *Journal of Criminal Justice*, 46 (2016): 55–65. https://doi.org/10.1016/j.jcrimjus.2016.03.008.

Black, Derek W. *Ending Zero Tolerance: The Crisis of Absolute School Discipline*. New York University Press, 2016.

Burch, Patricia. *System Failure: Policy and Practice in the School-to-Prison Pipeline*. 1st ed. Taylor and Francis, 2022.

Merkwae, Amanda. "Schooling the Police: Race, Disability, and the Conduct of School Resource Officers." *Michigan Journal of Race & Law*, 21 (2015): 147–58.

National Center for Education Statistics. "Indicators of School Crime and Safety: 2021." 2021. https://nces.ed.gov/pubs2022/2022006.pdf.

"The Overcriminalization of Youth in Our Public School Systems." *Juvenile Justice Update*, 21, no. 4 (2015).

Puzzanchera, Charles, Andrea Sladky, and Wei Kang. *Juvenile Justice Statistics: 1990–2021*, 2022. https://ojjdp.ojp.gov/publications/trends-in-youth-arrests.pdf.

Skiba, R. J., M. I. Arredondo, and N. T. Williams, "More than a Metaphor: The Contribution of Exclusionary Discipline to a School-to-Prison Pipeline." *Equity & Excellence in Education*, 47, no. 4 (2014): 546–64.

Tarescavage, Anthony M., Gary L. Fischler, Bruce M. Cappo, David O. Hill, David M. Corey, and Yossef S. Ben-Porath. "Minnesota Multiphasic Personality Inventory-2-Restructured Form (MMPI-2-RF) Predictors of Police Officer Problem Behavior and Collateral Self-Report Test Scores." *Psychological Assessment*, 27, no. 1 (2015): 125–37.

Texas Commission on Law Enforcement. 2023. https://www.tcole.texas.gov/.

Texas House Bill 3, 88th Leg., Reg. Sess. (Tex. 2023). Accessed December 13, 2023. https://capitol.texas.gov/BillLookup/History.aspx?LegSess=88R&Bill=HB3.

Theriot, Matthew T. "An Empirical Analysis of School Resource Officer Interactions with Students." *Journal of Criminal Justice,* 37, no. 3 (2009): 280–7. https://doi.org/10.1016/j.jcrimjus.

United States Census Bureau. "Age and Sex Composition in the United States: 2020." Accessed January 15, 2021. https://www.census.gov/data/tables/2020/demo/age-and-sex/2020-age-sex-composition.html.

Yarbrough, Jeffrey D. *Redefining School Safety and Policing: A Transformative Four Pillar Model.* Routledge, 2023.

Zahir, Kcyronne Q. "School Suspension Rates Among Minority Males and Leadership Styles of Principals: Analysis of the Relationship as Measured by Discipline Consequences." PhD. diss., ProQuest Dissertations Publishing, 2023.

3 Fostering a Culture of School Safety through Positive Relationships, Communication, Student Well-being and Engaging Parents and the Community

In today's ever-evolving educational landscape, ensuring the safety and well-being of students, staff, and parents is a primary concern for school and district administrators. Building a culture of school safety requires proactive efforts in fostering positive relationships and effective communication within the school community.

This chapter delves into evidence-based strategies and best practices that administrators can implement to promote a culture of safety through positive relationships and open communication. Creating a culture of safety in schools goes beyond physical security; it also encompasses fostering inclusivity and empowering students to actively participate in their own safety and the safety of their peers.

We will explore evidence-based strategies to promote inclusivity and empower students in building a safe school environment. Student well-being is a cornerstone of a thriving school community. As school and district administrators, it is crucial to prioritize the mental, emotional, and physical health of all students. This chapter delves into evidence-based strategies and best practices to promote student well-being, ensuring that every student has access to the necessary support and resources to flourish academically and personally.

In the dynamic landscape of modern education, the safety and well-being of students are paramount concerns for educators and administrators. To create a robust culture of safety, it is essential to engage parents and the broader community as valuable partners. This chapter also delves into the critical role of involving parents and community members in school safety efforts. By fostering collaboration, effective communication, and shared responsibility, schools can create a fortified safety network that extends beyond the classroom walls.

Promoting Positive Relationships

A positive school climate, grounded in trust and respect among staff, students, and parents, is essential for fostering a safe and nurturing educational environment. Building this foundation of mutual respect and understanding requires proactive efforts from school administrators, who can implement a range of evidence-based interventions and initiatives. These efforts should be informed by research and guided by experts in the field, ensuring that every member of the school community feels valued and supported. By prioritizing open communication, inclusivity, and collaborative problem-solving, administrators can create a culture where positive relationships flourish, ultimately enhancing the overall safety and well-being of the school community. Administrators can promote positive school relationships in the following ways:

Encouraging Regular Staff Collaborations

Fostering a collaborative culture among school staff is essential for not only addressing safety concerns but also for creating a secure and supportive learning environment. A strong, cohesive team can more effectively identify and resolve potential safety issues before they escalate, ensuring that all students are protected and cared for. Research by Mayer and Cornell underscores the importance of positive relationships among staff, noting that such connections can significantly reduce the need for exclusionary discipline practices, which often alienate students and exacerbate behavioral issues.[1]

Instead, a united staff can work together to implement more constructive approaches that improve student behavior and overall school climate.

To cultivate this culture of collaboration, administrators should prioritize organizing regular team meetings that go beyond routine discussions. These meetings should be structured to allow for open dialogue, brainstorming, and collective problem-solving, where every staff member feels heard and valued. Additionally, providing ongoing professional development opportunities specifically focused on safety, behavior management, and conflict resolution equips staff with the tools they need to handle challenges confidently and consistently. Encouraging cross-disciplinary collaborations is also crucial, as it brings together diverse perspectives and expertise, enriching the problem-solving process and fostering a sense of shared responsibility. By promoting unity and collective accountability, administrators can ensure that every staff member is not only engaged but also invested in creating and maintaining a safe, inclusive, and nurturing school environment.

Hosting Parent Engagement Events

Engaging parents as active partners in their children's education and safety is a cornerstone of fostering a positive and secure school climate. When parents are meaningfully involved, it not only strengthens the bond between home and school but also creates a unified approach to addressing challenges and supporting student success. The impact of a robust parent–school partnership, highlighting its potential to significantly reduce absenteeism and disciplinary issues, both of which are critical to maintaining a safe and productive learning environment.[2]

To build and strengthen this vital partnership, administrators should take proactive steps to host a variety of events that invite and encourage parents to engage actively in the school's safety initiatives. Informative workshops can provide parents with valuable insights into the safety protocols and procedures that the school has in place, ensuring they are well-informed and prepared to support these measures at home. Parenting seminars can offer strategies for fostering resilience, positive behavior, and academic success, reinforcing the school's efforts in creating a holistic support system for students. Additionally, community events that promote social interaction and collaboration can help bridge gaps between families, fostering a sense of unity and shared purpose within the school community. By creating these opportunities for meaningful engagement, administrators can cultivate a partnership where parents, staff, and students work together toward the common goal of a safe, nurturing, and supportive environment for every child.

Implementing Restorative Practices

Restorative practices offer a proactive and holistic approach to fostering positive relationships and effectively addressing conflicts within the school community. Unlike traditional disciplinary methods that often focus on punishment, restorative practices emphasize healing, accountability, and the restoration of relationships. These practices have shown to be highly effective in creating a safer and more inclusive school environment by promoting a culture of understanding and mutual respect.

By shifting the focus from punitive measures to constructive dialogue, restorative practices encourage students to take responsibility for their actions while also considering the impact of their behavior on others. This approach not only helps to resolve conflicts but also strengthens the overall sense of community within the school, reducing the likelihood of future incidents.

> Quick Tip: Building positive relationships with educators, staff, students, and parents is crucial, but extending this effort to develop strong, open connections with the local community is equally important. A close and collaborative relationship between the school and the community fosters trust, communication, and mutual support. The stronger this bond, the more engaged and active community members become in promoting and supporting school safety initiatives, creating a safer and more unified environment for everyone.

Administrators can introduce a variety of restorative practices tailored to the needs of their school. Restorative circles, for example, provide a structured yet flexible platform for students and staff to engage in open dialogue, share their perspectives, and work toward mutual understanding. This practice fosters a sense of belonging and safety, as everyone involved has an opportunity to be heard and valued. Peer mediation programs are another valuable tool, empowering students to take an active role in resolving conflicts among their peers in a constructive and respectful manner. Additionally, providing conflict resolution training for both students and staff can equip the entire school community with the skills necessary to handle disputes peacefully and effectively. By promoting empathy, accountability, and collaboration, restorative practices help build a cohesive school community where safety, respect, and positive relationships are foundational values

Effective Communication for School Safety

Transparent and effective communication is crucial for both preventing and addressing safety concerns within the school community. By employing evidence-based communication strategies, schools can ensure that all stakeholders—students, staff, parents, and the wider community—are well-informed and engaged in maintaining a safe environment. Key approaches to effective communication include evidence-based communication strategies and approaches include utilizing multiple communication channels

The National Association of School Psychologists underscores the critical need for using multiple communication channels to ensure that safety updates, policies, and emergency protocols reach all members of the school community effectively.[3]

In today's fast-paced and digitally connected world, relying on a single mode of communication is insufficient to guarantee that important information is received and understood by all stakeholders.

Administrators should therefore adopt a multifaceted approach to information dissemination, employing a variety of methods such as newsletters, emails, and the school website. Each of these channels serves a distinct purpose and audience, ensuring that every stakeholder—from staff and students to parents and community members—has access to the information they need to stay informed and prepared.

In addition to traditional communication methods, leveraging social media platforms is increasingly vital for enhancing connectivity and engagement within the school community. Social media offers a dynamic and immediate way to reach a broader audience, providing timely updates and fostering a sense of involvement among parents and students. By actively using platforms such as Facebook, Twitter, or Instagram, administrators can share real-time information, reminders, and safety alerts, ensuring that critical messages are disseminated quickly and efficiently. This comprehensive approach to communication not only enhances overall safety and preparedness but also strengthens the relationship between the school and its stakeholders. By utilizing a diverse array of communication tools, administrators can create a well-informed and cohesive community, better equipped to respond to any situation that may arise.

Implementing Anonymous Reporting Systems

The U.S. Secret Service and U.S. Department of Education highlight the pivotal role that anonymous reporting systems play in preventing targeted violence and ensuring the overall safety of school communities.[4]

These systems offer a secure and confidential avenue for students, staff, and even parents to report safety concerns without fear of retaliation or judgment.

By providing a mechanism where individuals can voice their concerns anonymously, schools are better equipped to identify and address potential threats before they have the chance to escalate into serious incidents. This proactive approach to safety not only helps to prevent violence but also builds trust within the school community, as everyone knows there is a safe way to report issues that might otherwise go unnoticed or unaddressed.

> Quick Tip: The value of robust reporting systems cannot be stressed highly enough. A comprehensive reporting platform should be a key part of any school safety program and should be well-integrated with the school's threat assessment team process. Make sure there is ample time to provide professional development training for staff on the reporting system and the process they will undertake in the case of an emergency.

To maximize the effectiveness of anonymous reporting systems, administrators must ensure that these tools are easily accessible and well-publicized throughout the school. Clear communication about how to use these systems and the importance of reporting concerns can foster a culture of vigilance and shared responsibility. Schools should integrate these reporting systems into their broader safety protocols, making it a routine part of how safety is maintained on campus. Additionally, regular reminders and updates about the availability and significance of these systems can help reinforce their importance and encourage ongoing use. By empowering students and staff to contribute to a safe and secure school environment through anonymous reporting, administrators can create a more vigilant and responsive community that prioritizes the well-being of all its members.

Conducting Regular Safety Drills and Training

The U.S. Department of Education underscores the critical importance of conducting regular safety drills and training to ensure that all members of the school community are thoroughly prepared to respond effectively in the event of an emergency.[5]

These drills are not just routine exercises; they are vital for embedding a culture of readiness and resilience within the school. By simulating various emergency scenarios—such as fire, lockdown, or natural disaster—students, staff, and even parents can gain a clear understanding of the actions required to ensure everyone's safety.

To maximize the effectiveness of these drills, administrators must communicate detailed instructions and provide comprehensive explanations of safety protocols. This includes ensuring that everyone knows their specific roles and responsibilities during a crisis, from teachers managing classroom evacuations to students knowing the safest routes to exit the building. Additionally, ongoing training sessions can be used to address any gaps in knowledge or to introduce new safety procedures as they are developed.

By regularly engaging the entire school community in these drills and training programs, administrators can foster a sense of preparedness and confidence. This proactive approach not only equips everyone with the necessary skills to handle emergencies but also reinforces the collective commitment to maintaining a safe and secure learning environment.

Promoting Inclusivity and Empowering Students in a Safe School Environment

Building a culture of safety in schools extends far beyond the implementation of physical security measures; it also requires fostering an environment of inclusivity and empowering students to take an active role in their own safety, as well as the safety of their peers. True school safety is achieved when every student feels valued, respected, and included, regardless of their background, identity, or abilities. By promoting inclusivity, schools can create a supportive atmosphere where diversity is celebrated, and every student has the opportunity to thrive.

There are a number of evidence-based strategies designed to promote inclusivity and empower students in cultivating a safe and welcoming school environment. These strategies include creating programs that encourage student leadership, peer mentoring, and collaborative problem-solving. By involving students in safety initiatives and decision-making processes, schools can give them a sense of ownership and responsibility for the well-being of their community. Additionally, implementing anti-bullying campaigns, promoting mental health awareness, and providing resources for marginalized groups are crucial steps in ensuring that all students feel safe and supported.

Empowering students to become advocates for their own safety and the safety of others not only strengthens the overall security of the school but also helps develop a generation of confident, responsible individuals who understand the importance of creating inclusive, safe spaces for everyone. This holistic approach to school safety recognizes that a secure environment is one where every student has the opportunity to contribute, feel heard, and be protected.

Creating a Sense of Belonging and Inclusivity

Establishing a school environment that celebrates diversity and ensures a sense of belonging for every student is vital for fostering a safe, supportive, and thriving atmosphere. When students feel accepted and valued for who they are, they are more likely to engage positively with their peers, contribute to the school community, and feel secure in their surroundings. A sense of belonging is not only fundamental to students' emotional well-being but also to the overall safety and cohesiveness of the school.

> **Covenant Presbyterian School, Nashville, Tennessee**
>
> On March 27, 2023, at approximately 10:13 a.m., an identified female/transgender male shooter, 28, armed with two rifles and a handgun, began shooting people inside and outside Covenant Presbyterian School in Nashville, Tennessee. Six people (three students and three faculty) were killed; one person (a law enforcement officer sustained incidental injuries) was wounded. The shooter was killed by law enforcement at the scene.
>
> www.fbi.gov

Figure 3.1. Covenent Presbyterian School, Tennessee. www.fbi.gov

To cultivate this inclusive environment, schools must actively implement evidence-based practices designed to promote diversity, equity, and inclusion. These practices might include developing curricula that reflect a wide range of cultural perspectives, ensuring that all students see themselves represented in the lessons they learn and the materials they study. Schools can also create programs that encourage cross-cultural exchanges, where students from different backgrounds have the opportunity to share their experiences and learn from one another.

Additionally, fostering a sense of belonging involves addressing and dismantling systemic barriers that may prevent certain groups of students from feeling fully included. This could involve revising school policies to ensure they are equitable, offering support services for students who face discrimination or bias, and providing professional development for staff to help them understand and address issues related to diversity and inclusion.

We will explore these and other evidence-based strategies for creating a school environment where every student feels a deep sense of belonging. By doing so, schools can build a foundation of trust and respect that not only enhances safety but also enriches the entire educational experience for all students.

Implementing Diversity and Inclusion Programs

Research by Benbenishty and Astor emphasizes the importance of understanding the broader ecological context—including cultural, organizational, and temporal factors—that affect school safety. This perspective suggests that fostering an inclusive and respectful school climate is crucial for preventing violence and promoting safety.[6]

These programs go beyond simple activities; they are integral to fostering a culture that celebrates cultural heritage, embraces differences, and promotes understanding among students and staff. Schools can integrate these values into the daily life of the school by organizing initiatives such as cultural awareness weeks, where students can explore and highlight the diverse cultures within the school community. International festivals that showcase global traditions, foods, and arts also offer powerful opportunities for students to engage with and appreciate the rich diversity of their peers.

In addition to these events, diversity workshops provide a deeper education on issues related to identity, such as race, ethnicity, and gender. These workshops help students and staff recognize and challenge biases, develop empathy, and improve communication across different backgrounds. By implementing these comprehensive programs, schools can create an environment where every student feels valued and included, enhancing both their social well-being and the overall safety and cohesion of the school community.

Providing Accessible Resources

Administrators play a crucial role in creating a school environment that is accessible and supportive of every student's unique needs. A commitment to inclusivity means recognizing and addressing the diverse challenges that students may face, whether they are English language learners, students with disabilities, or individuals from various cultural backgrounds. Providing accessible resources and tailored support for these students is not only a matter of equity but also a fundamental aspect of fostering a safe and inclusive learning environment. When students feel that their needs are understood and met, they are more likely to engage positively with their peers and educators, leading to a more cohesive and supportive school community.

To achieve this level of accessibility and support, administrators must take proactive steps to identify and remove barriers that may hinder any student's ability to thrive. This includes ensuring that educational materials, teaching strategies, and school facilities are adaptable and inclusive. For English language learners, providing language support services and culturally responsive teaching can help bridge communication gaps and make learning more effective. For students with disabilities, ensuring that classrooms and school resources are physically accessible and that individualized learning plans are in place can greatly enhance their educational experience. Additionally, fostering an environment that celebrates diversity and promotes cultural awareness helps all students feel valued and respected. By prioritizing accessibility and support, administrators can help cultivate a school culture where every student, regardless of their background or needs, feels safe, included, and empowered to succeed.

Encouraging Bystander Intervention and Reporting of Safety Concerns

Empowering students to become active bystanders who report safety concerns is a crucial strategy for cultivating a safe and secure school environment. When students understand the importance of speaking up and taking action when they witness potential threats or unsafe behavior, the entire school community benefits. Evidence-based strategies for fostering this sense of responsibility among students emphasize the need for comprehensive education and awareness campaigns. These initiatives should teach students about the impact of their actions, the importance of looking out for their peers, and the various ways they can report concerns safely and anonymously. By normalizing bystander intervention, schools can create a culture where students feel confident and supported in their efforts to contribute to the safety of their school.

To further encourage bystander intervention and reporting, administrators should implement a range of supportive measures and programs that reinforce these behaviors. This might include regular workshops or assemblies that educate students on recognizing signs of bullying, harassment, or other dangerous situations, as well as the appropriate steps to take when such incidents occur. Additionally, creating easily accessible reporting channels—such as anonymous tip lines, online reporting forms, or designated safe spaces where students can share their concerns—can make it easier for students to take action without fear of retaliation. Schools can also recognize and reward positive bystander behavior, highlighting students who have made a difference in maintaining a safe environment. By equipping students with the knowledge, tools, and confidence to intervene and report safety concerns, administrators can foster a proactive and vigilant school community where everyone plays a role in ensuring the well-being of their peers. Evidence-based strategies for encouraging bystander intervention and reporting include:

Implementing Anti-Bullying Campaigns

Anti-bullying campaigns are a vital component of fostering a safe and inclusive school environment, where every student feels valued and protected. Espelage and Swearer highlight the importance of these campaigns in empowering students to recognize and speak up against bullying behaviors, which can often go unnoticed or unreported.[7]

By implementing comprehensive anti-bullying initiatives, schools can create a culture of respect and empathy, where bullying is not tolerated, and students are encouraged to stand up for themselves and their peers. These campaigns can serve as both preventative and reactive measures, addressing the root causes of bullying while also providing support for those who may have been affected.

To be truly effective, anti-bullying campaigns should include a variety of educational sessions and activities designed to reach all members of the school community. Educational sessions can help students understand what constitutes bullying, how it affects individuals and the broader school climate, and the importance of taking a stand against such behaviors.

Promoting empathy is another key component, as fostering a sense of understanding and compassion among students can reduce the likelihood of bullying incidents and create a more supportive environment. Additionally, these campaigns should work toward cultivating a school culture where inclusivity and kindness are the norms. By involving not just students, but also teachers, staff, and parents in these efforts, schools can ensure a unified approach to preventing and addressing bullying, ultimately creating a safer, more positive learning environment for everyone.

Training Student Ambassadors

Training student ambassadors to serve as role models and safety advocates is an impactful strategy for enhancing the overall safety and well-being of the school community. Student ambassadors, who are typically well-respected by their peers, can play a pivotal role in promoting a positive school climate by setting an example of responsible and supportive behavior. According to Poteat and Espelage, when these students are trained to identify potential safety concerns and offer guidance to their peers, they contribute significantly to creating a safer and more inclusive environment.[8]

By empowering student ambassadors with the knowledge and skills needed to recognize and address issues such as bullying, harassment, and other forms of conflict, schools can extend their safety efforts beyond the administrative level and into the everyday interactions of students.

The training of student ambassadors should be comprehensive, covering not only the identification of safety concerns but also effective communication and conflict resolution techniques. This training equips ambassadors to provide peer support in a manner that is both compassionate and constructive, fostering a sense of trust and respect among students. Furthermore, student ambassadors can act as liaisons between the student body and school administration, helping to ensure that the concerns and needs of their peers are heard and addressed promptly. By involving students directly in the promotion of safety and well-being, schools can cultivate a climate where every student feels valued and protected. This peer-led approach not only enhances the effectiveness of safety initiatives but also reinforces the message that maintaining a safe and supportive environment is a shared responsibility.

> Quick Tip: Cultivating a school culture that prioritizes safety, security, and a shared sense of personal responsibility requires active buy-in from educators, staff, students, and the wider community. Achieving this goal demands ongoing collaboration, clear communication, and consistent effort from all stakeholders. To sustain this culture, it's essential to have a comprehensive onboarding plan for new staff members. Ensure they are fully informed about the initiatives in place to foster a positive and secure school environment, understand their role in supporting these efforts, and are equipped with the tools to contribute meaningfully. A well-integrated team strengthens the foundation of a supportive and safe school culture.

Publicizing Reporting Options

Effective communication about reporting options is crucial for ensuring that students feel comfortable and confident in coming forward with safety concerns. Clear and accessible information about how to report issues can significantly impact a student's willingness to share important safety-related information. According to the National Center for Safe Supportive Learning Environments, publicizing a range of reporting options—such as anonymous reporting systems, trusted staff members, and school counselors—is essential in creating an environment where students feel safe to voice their concerns.[9]

By making these reporting channels well-known and easily accessible, schools can help remove barriers that might otherwise discourage students from speaking up.

To effectively publicize reporting options, administrators should employ a variety of strategies to reach all students. This can include incorporating information into school orientations, distributing flyers, and regularly reminding students about reporting mechanisms during assemblies or class meetings. Additionally, ensuring that students understand the confidentiality and protection associated with anonymous reporting systems can further encourage them to report issues without fear of retaliation. By fostering an open and transparent communication environment, schools can create a culture where reporting safety concerns is viewed as a positive and responsible action. This approach not only empowers students to take an active role in maintaining a safe school environment but also enhances the overall effectiveness of safety protocols and interventions.

Educating and Empowering Students on Personal Safety and Awareness

Empowering students with knowledge and skills related to personal safety and awareness enhances their ability to protect themselves and others. Evidence-based strategies for educating and empowering students include:

Integrating Safety Education in Curriculum

Integrating safety education into the school curriculum is a crucial strategy for equipping students with the knowledge and skills necessary to navigate various safety challenges. According to research by the U.S. Department of Education, embedding safety topics such as internet safety, substance abuse prevention, and personal boundaries within the curriculum helps ensure that these important issues are addressed in a systematic and comprehensive manner.[10]

By incorporating these topics into relevant subjects, students receive practical, age-appropriate education that is directly applicable to their daily lives. This approach not only raises awareness but also provides students with actionable strategies to protect themselves and make informed decisions.

To effectively integrate safety education, administrators and educators should collaborate to identify natural connections between safety topics and existing curriculum areas. For instance, internet safety lessons can be woven into technology or computer science classes, while substance abuse prevention can be included in health education or physical education courses. Personal boundaries and consent can be discussed within social studies or physical education contexts. Additionally, providing professional development for teachers on how to effectively deliver safety education can enhance its impact. By making safety education a seamless part of the learning experience, schools can foster a culture of awareness and preparedness, ensuring that students are well-equipped to handle safety concerns both in and out of school.

Hosting Workshops and Seminars

Organizing workshops and seminars led by experts in the field is a powerful way to equip students with essential knowledge and resources that promote safety and well-being. These events provide an opportunity to delve deeply into critical topics such as cyber safety, mental health awareness, and healthy relationships—areas that are increasingly important in today's complex world. By bringing in professionals who specialize in these subjects, schools can offer students a comprehensive understanding of the challenges they may face and the tools they need to navigate them effectively. These workshops can be tailored to address the specific needs and concerns of the student body, ensuring that the information is both relevant and practical.

Quick Tip: Integrating opportunities for students to learn and practice critical decision-making skills into their school experience has far-reaching benefits. These skills not only prepare students to navigate complex challenges but also foster better outcomes in their personal and social interactions, positively impacting everyone they encounter. Whether responding to a traffic collision, a sports injury, or any other emergency, the ability to assess situations, make sound decisions, and act effectively can make a significant difference in the outcome. By teaching these essential skills, we empower students to thrive in real-world situations.

In addition to the immediate educational benefits, hosting workshops and seminars can also foster a culture of continuous learning and proactive engagement with safety and wellness issues. These events encourage students to ask questions, seek help, and discuss important topics openly, which can lead to greater awareness and resilience. Furthermore, involving parents and community members in these sessions can extend the impact beyond the school, creating a supportive network that reinforces the lessons learned. By regularly offering these educational opportunities, schools can ensure that students are not only informed but also empowered to take an active role in their own safety and well-being, ultimately contributing to a more secure and supportive school environment.

Promoting Social Emotional Learning

Promoting Social Emotional Learning (SEL) is essential for fostering students' emotional intelligence, empathy, and conflict resolution skills, all of which are crucial for creating a positive and supportive school environment. SEL programs focus on helping students develop self-awareness, manage their emotions, build strong relationships, and make responsible decisions. According to the American School Counselor Association, incorporating SEL into the curriculum enhances students' social and emotional competencies, which directly contributes to a safer school atmosphere.[11]

By teaching these skills, schools not only address students' academic needs but also equip them with the tools to navigate interpersonal challenges and maintain healthy relationships with peers and adults.

The integration of SEL into the curriculum has far-reaching benefits that extend beyond the classroom. As students become more adept at understanding and managing their emotions, they are better prepared to handle conflicts constructively, reducing the likelihood of violence or bullying. Additionally, SEL programs can promote a culture of empathy and respect, where students are more likely to support one another and contribute to a positive school climate.

Schools that prioritize SEL create an environment where students feel valued, understood, and connected, which is foundational for both their academic success and overall well-being. By consistently promoting SEL, educators can help develop well-rounded individuals who are not only academically competent but also emotionally resilient and socially responsible, leading to a safer and more harmonious school community.

Mental health is a critical component of overall student well-being and can greatly impact student and staff safety within schools. Administrators can support mental health through a number of ways which include:

Collaborating with School Counselors and Psychologists

Collaborating with school counselors and psychologists is crucial for creating a comprehensive support system that addresses the mental health and well-being of students. These professionals are uniquely equipped to provide the specialized care and guidance that students may need, particularly when they face emotional or psychological challenges. By working closely with school counselors and psychologists, administrators can ensure that students who require intervention are identified early and connected with the appropriate resources and services. This collaborative approach allows for a more proactive and preventative stance on mental health, reducing the likelihood of issues escalating into more serious concerns. Goodman-Scott et al. emphasize the importance of such partnerships in fostering a school environment where every student feels supported and understood.[12]

In addition to identifying students in need, administrators and mental health professionals can work together to develop individualized intervention plans tailored to each student's specific needs. This process involves assessing the unique circumstances and challenges faced by the student and creating a plan that provides targeted support, whether through counseling, peer support groups, or external services. By ensuring that these plans are implemented effectively, schools can address the diverse emotional and psychological needs of their students. Moreover, regular communication between administrators, counselors, and psychologists is essential to monitor progress and make necessary adjustments to intervention strategies. This ongoing collaboration not only enhances the well-being of individual students but also contributes to a more positive and inclusive school culture where mental health is prioritized, and all students are given the opportunity to thrive.

Utilizing Telehealth Services for Student Mental Health

Telehealth services have emerged as a vital resource for providing convenient and accessible mental health support to students, particularly those in rural or underserved areas where in-person counseling options may be limited. With the rise of digital platforms like "BetterHelp" and "Talkspace," students now have the opportunity to connect with licensed mental health professionals from the comfort and privacy of their homes. This accessibility is crucial in reducing barriers to mental health care, allowing students to receive the

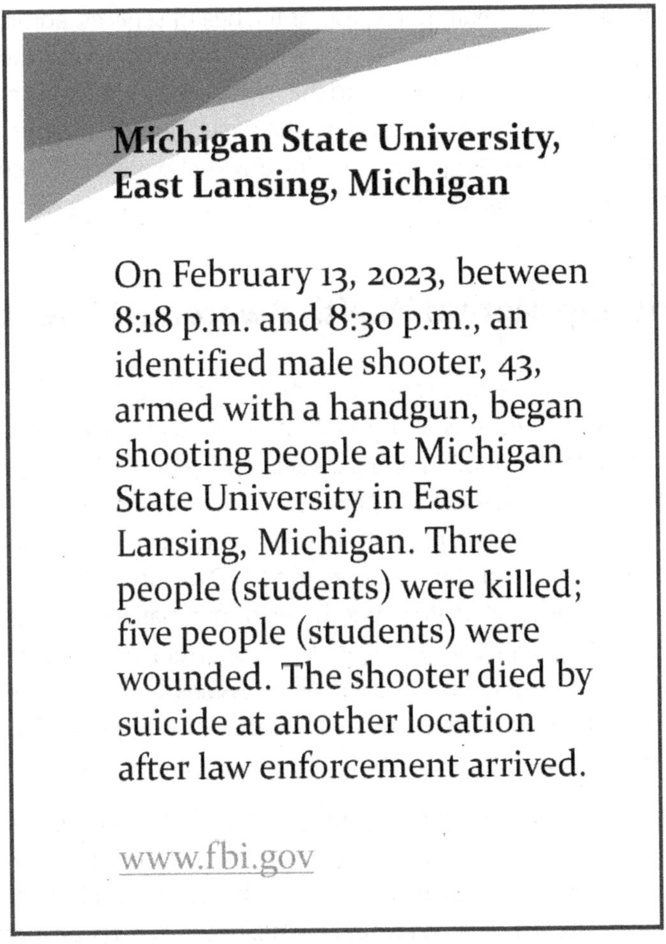

> **Michigan State University, East Lansing, Michigan**
>
> On February 13, 2023, between 8:18 p.m. and 8:30 p.m., an identified male shooter, 43, armed with a handgun, began shooting people at Michigan State University in East Lansing, Michigan. Three people (students) were killed; five people (students) were wounded. The shooter died by suicide at another location after law enforcement arrived.
>
> www.fbi.gov

Figure 3.2. Michigan State University. www.fbi.gov

support they need without the added stress of travel or scheduling conflicts. These platforms offer flexible options, including text, video, and phone sessions, which cater to the varying needs and preferences of students, making mental health care more adaptable to their lifestyles.

Administrators can play a pivotal role in expanding the reach of these services by collaborating with mental health organizations that specialize in telehealth. Establishing partnerships with these organizations can help integrate telehealth services into the school's existing support system, providing students with additional avenues for seeking help. Schools can also consider offering telehealth access through designated school spaces for students who may not have the privacy or technology required at home. By promoting and facilitating the use of telehealth services, administrators can ensure that every student, regardless of their geographic location or personal circumstances, has access to the mental health care they need. This proactive approach not only enhances the well-being of students but also contributes to a more supportive and inclusive school environment where mental health is prioritized.

Promoting Mental Health Awareness Events

Promoting mental health awareness through events such as mental health fairs, guest speaker sessions, and workshops is an effective way to encourage open conversations about mental health and reduce the stigma often associated with it. These events provide a platform for students, staff, and parents to engage in meaningful discussions about mental health issues, self-care strategies, and the resources available to support those in need. Mental health fairs can feature booths with information on local mental health services, interactive activities, and opportunities to connect with mental health professionals. Guest speaker sessions can bring in experts or individuals with lived experiences to share their stories, providing valuable insights and fostering empathy within the school community.

Administrators can further enhance the impact of these events by partnering with organizations like "Mental Health America," which offers a wealth of resources and toolkits designed to help schools effectively host mental health awareness activities. By inviting mental health experts, advocates, and community members to participate, these events can become a central part of the school's efforts to promote mental health education. Workshops focused on specific topics, such as stress management, anxiety, or the importance of self-care, can provide practical tools and strategies that students, staff, and parents can use in their daily lives. In doing so, these events not only raise awareness but also empower the entire school community to take an active role in supporting mental health, ultimately contributing to a more informed, compassionate, and resilient school environment.

Implementing Effective Crisis Intervention and Counseling Support

Being prepared for crises is essential for maintaining a safe and supportive school environment. Administrators can implement crisis intervention and counseling support by:

Creating Crisis Response Teams

Establishing crisis response teams within schools is a critical measure to ensure a coordinated and effective response to emergencies. These teams, composed of counselors, psychologists, teachers, and administrators, are essential for managing crises such as natural disasters, acts of violence, or other unforeseen emergencies that can significantly impact the school community. By bringing together professionals with diverse expertise, schools can create a multidisciplinary approach to crisis management, ensuring that all aspects of a situation are addressed—from the immediate safety of students and staff to the longer-term psychological support required for recovery. The National Center for School Crisis and Bereavement provides invaluable guidelines and resources for developing these teams, offering best practices that schools can adapt to their specific needs and circumstances.[13]

However, simply establishing crisis response teams is not enough; these teams must be regularly trained and equipped to handle the wide range of potential crises they may face. Administrators have a crucial role in ensuring that crisis response teams participate in ongoing professional development, which should include simulated drills, workshops on crisis communication, and training on the latest emergency management strategies. Regular training is essential not only for maintaining the readiness of the teams but also for adapting to new challenges, such as the increasing complexity of crises in today's world. For instance, in addition to traditional emergencies like natural disasters, schools must now be prepared to address crises related to cyber threats, mental health crises, and even global pandemics. By investing in the continuous education and preparedness of crisis response teams, administrators can significantly enhance the school's ability to protect and support its community during critical moments, fostering a safer and more resilient school environment.[14]

Implementing Trauma-Informed Practices

Implementing trauma-informed practices within schools is essential for creating an environment that recognizes and supports students who have experienced trauma. Trauma can have a profound impact on a student's ability to learn, form relationships, and feel safe within the school setting. By adopting trauma-informed practices, schools can foster an atmosphere of understanding and compassion, where students feel acknowledged and supported in their emotional and psychological needs. The Substance Abuse and Mental Health Services Administration (SAMHSA) provides a comprehensive guide for educators on implementing a trauma-informed approach, which includes principles such as safety, trustworthiness, peer support, and empowerment.[15]

These principles serve as the foundation for creating a school culture that is sensitive to the challenges faced by students affected by trauma.

To effectively integrate trauma-informed practices, it is crucial for administrators to facilitate thorough training for all school staff, including teachers, counselors, and support personnel. This training should equip staff with the knowledge and skills necessary to recognize signs of trauma and to respond in ways that do not re-traumatize students but rather help them feel safe and understood. Trauma-informed training can cover a range of topics, such as understanding the effects of trauma on behavior and learning, implementing strategies for de-escalation, and fostering positive relationships that build trust with students. Additionally, this training should encourage staff to adopt a mindset that views challenging behaviors as potential expressions of trauma, rather than simply disciplinary issues. By shifting the perspective of staff toward a more empathetic and supportive approach, schools can create an environment that not only addresses the academic needs of students but also their emotional well-being.

Beyond training, ongoing support and resources are necessary to sustain trauma-informed practices within the school community. Administrators should ensure that staff have access to continuous professional development opportunities that deepen their understanding of trauma and its impact on students. This might include regular workshops, peer discussions, and access to resources that offer the latest research and strategies in trauma-informed care. Moreover, it's important to create systems within the school that allow for consistent monitoring and support of trauma-informed practices, such as regular check-ins with staff, collaborative problem-solving sessions, and a clear communication plan for addressing trauma-related issues. By embedding these practices into the fabric of the school, administrators can help create a compassionate and resilient educational environment where all students, particularly those affected by trauma, can thrive.[16]

Collaborating with Local Crisis Hotlines

Collaborating with local crisis hotlines and mental health organizations is a critical step in providing immediate and accessible support for students and staff during times of crisis. These partnerships enable schools to offer timely counseling services that can be crucial in preventing or mitigating the impact of emergencies on the school community. Crisis hotlines like the Crisis Text Line (Text "HOME" to 741741) and the National Suicide Prevention Lifeline (1-800-273-TALK) provide 24/7 support, offering a lifeline to individuals in distress. By establishing strong connections with these resources, schools can ensure that students, parents, and staff have direct access to professional mental health support whenever they need it. Additionally, these partnerships allow schools to tap into a broader network of mental health professionals who can offer specialized assistance, helping to address complex issues that may arise during crises.

To maximize the effectiveness of these collaborations, administrators should actively promote the availability of these crisis hotlines through various school communication channels. This includes disseminating information via newsletters, school websites, social media platforms, and even posters in common areas around the school. Ensuring that everyone in the school community is aware of these resources can empower students, parents, and staff to seek help when needed, potentially averting crises before they escalate. Moreover, regular reminders and updates about these services can keep the lines of communication open, fostering a school environment where mental health and well-being are prioritized. By integrating the promotion of crisis hotlines into the school's broader mental health strategy, administrators can help build a supportive network that extends beyond the school walls, ensuring that the entire community has access to vital support systems in times of need.

Encouraging Social Emotional Learning and Resilience-Building Programs Social Emotional Learning (SEL) is key to nurturing students' emotional intelligence and resilience. Administrators can promote SEL and resilience-building through:

Implementing SEL Curricula

Implementing Social Emotional Learning (SEL) curricula is a pivotal strategy for fostering a positive and supportive school climate. SEL programs, such as those offered by the Collaborative for Academic, Social, and Emotional Learning (CASEL), are designed to enhance students' self-awareness, self-management, social awareness, relationship skills, and responsible decision-making. These evidence-based curricula provide structured and proven approaches to developing students' social-emotional competencies, which are crucial for their overall well-being and academic success. By integrating SEL into the school curriculum, educators can help students build essential life skills that support their emotional and social growth. This not only improves individual student outcomes but also contributes to a more cohesive and respectful school environment where students are better equipped to navigate interpersonal challenges and manage their emotions effectively.[17]

Beyond the classroom, the implementation of SEL curricula can have far-reaching benefits for the entire school community. Schools that adopt SEL programs often see improvements in student behavior, reductions in bullying and disciplinary issues, and enhanced academic performance. Additionally, SEL helps to create a culture of empathy and collaboration, where students are encouraged to support one another and engage in positive relationships. For successful implementation, administrators should ensure that SEL curricula are integrated seamlessly into daily activities and lessons, and that teachers receive adequate training and support to effectively deliver these programs. By embedding SEL into the fabric of the school's educational approach, administrators can cultivate a nurturing environment where students are empowered to develop both their academic and emotional capabilities, paving the way for a more harmonious and productive school experience.

Offering Peer Support Programs

Implementing peer support programs, such as "Sources of Strength," is a proactive way to create a school culture where students support and uplift one another during challenging times. These programs empower students to be key players in promoting mental health, emotional well-being, and resilience within their peer groups. By training student leaders to recognize signs of distress and offer constructive guidance, peer support initiatives can foster a sense of connectedness and belonging among students, which is essential for creating a safe and inclusive school environment. These programs help reduce the stigma surrounding mental health issues and encourage open conversations, making it easier for students to seek help when they need it.

Research by Wyman et al. indicates that peer-led support programs are particularly effective in improving students' overall emotional well-being and promoting a more cohesive school community.[18]

To establish and sustain successful peer support programs, administrators must actively collaborate with both student leaders and school staff. This includes selecting students who are well-respected by their peers and providing them with proper training on how to offer emotional support, recognize warning signs of crises, and refer students to professional help when necessary. In addition to training, administrators should ensure ongoing supervision and support for student leaders, allowing them to thrive in their roles without feeling overwhelmed. Regular meetings, workshops, and feedback sessions can help refine the program, ensuring its effectiveness. Moreover, promoting inclusivity and diversity within peer support groups is crucial, as it allows students from different backgrounds to feel represented and heard. By fostering a culture of mutual respect and understanding through peer support programs, schools can create a safe, supportive atmosphere where every student feels valued and empowered.

Providing Mindfulness Practices

Integrating mindfulness practices into the school environment offers students effective tools to manage stress, regulate emotions, and develop healthier coping mechanisms. Techniques such as meditation, breathing exercises, and mindful reflection help students become more aware of their thoughts and feelings, fostering greater emotional resilience. Programs and resources from organizations like "Mindful Schools" and "Mindful.org" provide valuable guidance for implementing these practices within the school setting. By practicing mindfulness regularly, students can develop a sense of calm and focus, which positively impacts both their emotional well-being and academic performance. Research by Zhang et al. highlights the benefits of mindfulness in reducing stress and anxiety, promoting a more peaceful and attentive school climate.[19]

> Quick Tip: Creating opportunities to teach and nurture resilience in both students and staff is essential to building a positive and supportive school culture. Partnering with public safety and mental health agencies to bring their expertise into resilience development not only strengthens the school environment but also extends these benefits to the broader community. By fostering resilience, we equip individuals with the tools to overcome challenges, adapt to change, and contribute to a healthier, more connected society.

To effectively incorporate mindfulness into the school day, administrators can allocate specific time for mindful activities, such as short meditation sessions at the beginning of class or mindfulness breaks during transitions. Providing teachers with professional development opportunities focused on mindfulness techniques is also essential, ensuring they are equipped to lead students through these exercises confidently. In addition, schools can create designated mindfulness spaces, such as quiet rooms or outdoor areas, where students can engage in mindful reflection when needed. By embedding mindfulness practices into the school culture, administrators can support students' mental health and foster a more supportive and balanced environment, where both academic success and emotional well-being are prioritized.

Addressing substance abuse by students and implementing substance abuse prevention is vital for student well-being and overall school safety. Administrators can take the following measures at their schools to help ensure student safety and address any substance abuse issues they may be having at their school sites.

Implementing Evidence-Based Prevention Programs

Integrating evidence-based prevention programs into the school curriculum is an essential strategy for empowering students to resist substance abuse and make healthier, informed choices. Programs such as "Botvin LifeSkills Training" and "Project ALERT" offer research-backed approaches to equip students with the knowledge and skills necessary to avoid the pitfalls of substance use. These programs go beyond simply warning students about the dangers of drugs and alcohol; they emphasize building critical life skills such as decision-making, coping strategies, peer resistance techniques, and effective communication. By incorporating these programs into health education classes or after-school activities, administrators can ensure that students are not only aware of the risks but are also equipped with practical tools to handle peer pressure and stressful situations that might lead to substance use.

Incorporating programs like "Botvin LifeSkills Training," which focuses on building personal and social competencies, helps students develop self-esteem and learn to manage anxiety—key factors in reducing the likelihood of substance abuse. Similarly, "Project ALERT" is designed to increase students' awareness of the social influences that encourage drug use, while teaching them how to confidently resist those pressures. Administrators can further expand the reach of these programs by organizing workshops, school-wide assemblies, or after-school clubs that focus on substance abuse prevention.[20]

Bringing in health professionals or individuals with personal stories of overcoming addiction as guest speakers can also serve to reinforce the program's messages in a more relatable and impactful way.

By combining these evidence-based programs with additional resources such as "D.A.R.E." (Drug Abuse Resistance Education) and "Too Good for Drugs," schools can provide a multilayered approach to prevention that engages students at various levels. Involving parents through informational seminars and workshops can further extend the reach of these initiatives, ensuring a consistent message is delivered at both school and home. Creating peer-led discussions or support groups, where students can engage in open conversations about the challenges they face, also promotes an inclusive environment where prevention and support go hand in hand. This holistic, evidence-based approach enables schools to not only prevent substance abuse but also to foster a healthier, more resilient student body prepared to make sound choices for their futures.

Offering Substance Abuse Counseling

Providing substance abuse counseling within schools is an essential step toward supporting students struggling with addiction and preventing further harm. School counselors and psychologists play a pivotal role in addressing the emotional, psychological, and behavioral challenges that often accompany substance abuse. These professionals can offer one-on-one counseling, group therapy sessions, and crisis interventions, helping students navigate their way toward recovery. Schools can collaborate with organizations like the National Institute on Drug Abuse (NIDA), which offers valuable resources on effective counseling and intervention strategies. By integrating these services into the school setting, administrators ensure that students have access to immediate and confidential support, making it easier for them to seek help without fear of stigma or punishment.

Administrators should also focus on creating a supportive and nonpunitive environment, where students struggling with substance abuse feel safe to come forward and ask for help. Schools can implement confidential referral systems, allowing teachers, staff, or peers to refer students in need of counseling. In conjunction with programs like "D.A.R.E." and "Too Good for Drugs," which educate students about substance abuse, providing in-house counseling ensures that schools are equipped to offer both prevention and intervention services. By offering individualized counseling and support plans tailored to each student's needs, school counselors and psychologists can help students develop coping mechanisms, build resilience, and make positive choices for their futures. Additionally, creating peer support networks and connecting students to community-based services further enhances the overall approach to combating substance abuse within the school community.

Collaborating with Community Anti-Drug Coalitions

Collaborating with community anti-drug coalitions is a powerful way for schools to enhance their substance abuse prevention and intervention efforts. By working with organizations like the Community Anti-Drug Coalitions of America (CADCA), schools can tap into local resources, expertise, and support networks that extend beyond the campus. These partnerships provide schools with access to evidence-based strategies and programs that have been proven effective in addressing substance abuse within communities. CADCA offers guidance on how to build and maintain anti-drug coalitions, helping schools develop a comprehensive approach to substance abuse prevention that involves students, parents, educators, and local leaders. By forming alliances with community coalitions, schools are able to foster a collective sense of responsibility and support in addressing the challenges of drug abuse.

In addition to benefiting from shared resources, collaborating with community anti-drug coalitions also allows schools to create targeted prevention programs that are tailored to the specific needs of their student population. Schools can work closely with coalition members to organize community events, workshops, and outreach initiatives that raise awareness about the dangers of drug use and provide students with the tools to make healthy choices. These partnerships also allow for the pooling of resources to provide more comprehensive services, such as access to drug counseling, treatment options, and support networks for students struggling with addiction. Through collaboration with anti-drug coalitions, schools can extend their influence and create a robust network of support that surrounds students with positive reinforcement and preventive education both inside and outside the school environment.

Moreover, community coalitions can serve as a bridge between schools and local law enforcement, healthcare providers, and social services, facilitating a coordinated effort in combating substance abuse. This multiagency collaboration ensures that students not only receive prevention education but also have access to timely intervention and recovery services when needed. Schools can play an active role in coalition activities by contributing data on student needs, participating in planning efforts, and promoting joint initiatives that engage the entire community in the fight against drug abuse. By leveraging the strengths of community anti-drug coalitions, schools become key players in a larger movement to create safe, drug-free environments where students can learn, grow, and thrive.

Supporting the unique needs of all students is critical for school safety and the well-being of all students. Administrators can provide support in the following six ways.

Establishing Safe Spaces and Support Groups

Establishing safe spaces and support groups within schools is essential for fostering a sense of belonging and emotional support, particularly for vulnerable populations. Students who identify as LGBTQ+, those from diverse racial and cultural backgrounds, or those experiencing personal challenges can greatly benefit from having designated areas where they feel secure, valued, and heard. These spaces serve as refuge for students, providing them with a supportive environment where they can express themselves openly without fear of judgment or discrimination. Organizations like GLSEN offer valuable resources for creating safe and inclusive spaces specifically tailored to LGBTQ+ students, guiding schools in promoting acceptance and understanding. By collaborating with student organizations, administrators can ensure that these spaces are responsive to the unique needs of various student populations, helping to cultivate a school culture that prioritizes emotional well-being, respect, and inclusion.

In addition to physical safe spaces, schools can establish support groups that provide a platform for students to connect with others who share similar experiences and challenges. Support groups offer peer-driven discussions facilitated by trained staff, enabling students to share their thoughts and concerns in a structured yet compassionate setting. Administrators can partner with community organizations to create and sustain these groups, ensuring they are equipped with professional guidance and resources. These initiatives not only offer students emotional support but also promote resilience and self-advocacy. By providing safe spaces and support groups, schools affirm their commitment to inclusivity, allowing vulnerable students to thrive academically and socially while contributing to a school culture that celebrates diversity and mutual respect.

Offering Community-Based Support Services

Connecting vulnerable students with community-based support services is an essential strategy to ensure that they have access to resources that go beyond what the school can provide. Many students face challenges that require more specialized or ongoing support, such as counseling, mentoring, or access to basic needs, that schools alone may not be able to fully address. Partnering with community-based organizations, such as counseling centers and local support networks, allows schools to offer a more comprehensive safety net for students who are at risk. For example, the "Big Brothers Big Sisters" organization provides mentoring programs specifically designed for at-risk youth, pairing them with adult mentors who offer guidance, emotional support, and encouragement. By connecting students to such programs, schools can help foster strong, positive relationships that may significantly impact their academic and personal development.

Administrators play a vital role in facilitating these connections by actively partnering with local organizations and establishing referral systems that make it easy for students and families to access needed services. This collaboration extends the support network for students, ensuring they are cared for in a holistic manner that addresses not only their educational needs but also their emotional, social, and developmental well-being as well. By building strong partnerships with community-based organizations, schools create a bridge between the academic environment and the wider community, helping students navigate difficult circumstances with a broader range of resources. These collaborations can significantly enhance the overall well-being of vulnerable students, fostering resilience, stability, and a sense of belonging both within and outside the school environment.

> Quick Tip: Integrating evidence-based prevention programs into the school curriculum is a powerful way to equip students with the skills and knowledge to resist substance abuse and make informed choices. Programs like "Botvin LifeSkills Training" and "Project ALERT" focus on building critical life skills such as decision-making, coping strategies, and peer resistance techniques, going beyond just warnings about drugs and alcohol. By combining these initiatives with partnerships involving parents, health professionals, and community organizations, schools can create a multilayered approach to prevention that fosters resilience and empowers students to make healthier decisions for life.

Establishing Partnerships with Parents and Families to Promote Safety

Building strong partnerships between schools and parents is a vital component of a comprehensive school safety strategy. When parents are actively engaged in the safety planning process, it fosters a sense of shared responsibility and trust, creating a more cohesive and secure school environment. Research indicates that involving parents in safety discussions and decision-making not only enhances communication but also improves the effectiveness of safety initiatives.[21]

Open lines of communication are essential to this collaboration, allowing both school staff and parents to share concerns, exchange ideas, and remain informed about ongoing safety efforts. This partnership ensures that parents feel included and valued in the process, contributing to a more unified approach to addressing safety concerns.

Administrators can foster this collaboration by hosting safety-focused events such as workshops, town hall meetings, and parent advisory boards. These gatherings allow parents to contribute directly to the development and implementation of safety measures, offering valuable insights and suggestions based on their unique perspectives. Regular workshops can also educate parents on critical safety protocols and practices, ensuring that families are informed and aligned with the school's objectives. Parent advisory boards provide an additional platform for ongoing dialogue, allowing administrators and parents to co-create solutions that are tailored to the specific needs and challenges of the school community. By fostering these partnerships, schools can build a culture of safety that extends beyond the classroom, ensuring that all stakeholders are working together to protect and support students.

Communicating Safety Protocols and Updates Effectively

Clear, consistent communication is a cornerstone of effective school safety management. It is critical that administrators ensure parents, students, and staff are well-informed about safety protocols, emergency procedures, and any relevant updates. Research underscores the importance of utilizing multiple communication channels to reach the entire school community effectively. Digital platforms such as school websites, social media, and email newsletters allow for timely dissemination of information, while printed newsletters and community forums offer more traditional means of communication for those less digitally inclined.[22]

By diversifying communication methods, schools can ensure that safety information reaches all stakeholders, no matter their preferred medium.

Aligning communication strategies with best practices set forth by organizations such as the National Association of School Resource Officers (NASRO) helps to ensure that messaging is clear, precise, and designed to enhance overall school security.[23]

Administrators should prioritize transparency when communicating safety measures, providing regular updates to parents and staff to foster trust and a sense of security. In addition, conducting regular drills and meetings to review emergency protocols further reinforces these safety messages and ensures everyone is prepared in the event of a crisis. By maintaining open, accessible, and proactive communication, schools can build a well-informed community, ready to respond effectively to any safety challenges that may arise.

Encouraging Parental Involvement in Safety Committees and Initiatives

Parental involvement in safety committees and initiatives is a powerful way to strengthen the overall effectiveness of school safety measures. When parents are actively engaged in decision-making processes, they bring valuable perspectives and concerns that can help shape comprehensive safety strategies. Schools can establish safety committees that bring together parents, teachers, administrators, and community members, creating a collaborative space for assessing risks, developing safety plans, and evaluating their execution.[24]

This collective approach ensures that safety initiatives are well-rounded and responsive to the needs of the entire school community.

Involving parents in these efforts fosters a sense of shared responsibility and ownership in maintaining a secure environment. By working alongside school staff and other stakeholders, parents become not only advocates but also active participants in ensuring the safety of their children. Schools can further encourage parental involvement by hosting workshops and information sessions that educate parents on current safety protocols and procedures, giving them the knowledge and tools to contribute meaningfully. This partnership strengthens the bond between home and school, reinforcing the community's commitment to creating a safe, supportive learning environment for all students.

Collaborating with Community Organizations and Resources for Support

Effective school safety goes beyond the walls of the school and involves actively partnering with community organizations and resources. Collaborating with local law enforcement agencies, fire departments, and health organizations not only enhances emergency response coordination but also strengthens the overall safety infrastructure. Research highlights the importance of these partnerships, noting that working with community-based organizations like the Red Cross or mental health providers helps ensure a holistic approach to school safety.[25]

By forming these connections, schools can access a broader range of expertise, support, and resources that directly contribute to a safer learning environment.

Administrators can take an active role in facilitating these collaborations through joint training sessions, workshops, and safety drills that involve both school staff and community partners.

This alignment of practices ensures that everyone is prepared to respond cohesively in the event of an emergency. Additionally, these collaborations provide opportunities to address other aspects of student well-being, such as mental health, through resources offered by community organizations. By building strong relationships with external partners, schools not only improve their immediate crisis response capabilities but also create a network of support that enhances safety and well-being for students, staff, and families.

> Quick Tip: Partnering with parents and families is essential for creating a safe and cohesive school environment. Engage parents in safety planning through workshops, advisory boards, and open communication to foster trust and a shared sense of responsibility. By working together, schools and families can build a stronger, more unified approach to student safety.

Conclusion

Building a culture of school safety through positive relationships and communication is a multifaceted and ongoing endeavor that requires intentional and sustained efforts from school administrators. Creating a supportive learning environment begins with fostering strong, trusting relationships between staff, students, and parents. Effective communication is equally crucial; it ensures that everyone is informed, engaged, and aligned with the school's safety goals.

Administrators play a pivotal role in promoting this culture by adopting evidence-based practices and interventions, which serve as the backbone of a safety-focused environment. These initiatives not only protect the school community but also enhance the overall well-being of every individual within

It. By prioritizing relationships and clear communication, administrators set the stage for a school culture where safety and support are deeply embedded in every aspect of the educational experience.

In addition, fostering inclusivity and empowering students to actively contribute to a safe school environment is key to building a thriving educational community. This effort requires the collective commitment of administrators, educators, students, and the wider community. By implementing evidence-based strategies, such as promoting a sense of belonging and encouraging bystander intervention, administrators ensure that students are not only physically safe but also feel emotionally supported. Educating and empowering students to take ownership of their safety and that of their peers reinforces the idea that everyone has a role to play. When a school environment is truly inclusive and supportive, students are more likely to flourish, both academically and socially. In creating this foundation, administrators help students cultivate positive lifelong skills, setting them up for long-term success in all areas of their lives.

Promoting student well-being is not just about academic achievement; it is about fostering a holistic approach that addresses emotional, social, and mental health needs. School and district administrators are integral to this process, as they must ensure that comprehensive support systems are in place. These systems include access to mental health services, crisis intervention measures, and Social Emotional Learning (SEL) programs that teach students essential life skills like empathy, self-awareness, and conflict resolution. By addressing critical issues like substance abuse and providing specialized support for vulnerable student populations, administrators create an environment where every student can feel safe, valued, and supported. This inclusive approach lays the groundwork for a nurturing school climate that prioritizes the well-being of every individual.

Adopting evidence-based strategies and leveraging real-world resources such as telehealth services, community partnerships, and SEL curricula empowers students to thrive both academically and emotionally. Administrators who champion these initiatives are not only providing short-term benefits but are also equipping students with the tools they need for long-term success. By fostering a school culture that emphasizes mental health, inclusivity, and proactive support, administrators create a positive, nurturing environment that benefits students, staff, and the larger school community alike. These efforts result in better academic performance, improved emotional resilience, and a more harmonious school experience for all.

Engaging parents and the broader community in school safety initiatives is a vital step toward transforming safety from a school-centric concern into a shared, collective responsibility. When schools actively partner with parents, they create an inclusive atmosphere where parents feel empowered to contribute to the safety and well-being of their children. This partnership fosters open communication, shared decision-making, and mutual trust. By hosting safety-focused workshops, parent advisory boards, and town hall meetings, schools offer parents the opportunity to voice concerns, offer insights, and collaborate on creating tailored safety measures that suit the unique needs of the school community. These efforts promote transparency and ensure that parents are informed and engaged in all aspects of school safety.

Collaboration with community organizations further strengthens the safety framework, ensuring that schools have access to a range of external resources and expertise. Whether partnering with local law enforcement, mental health organizations, or fire departments, schools benefit from having strong, coordinated support systems in place. Research has shown that when schools and communities work together, safety efforts become more comprehensive, proactive, and effective. Administrators can lead the way by organizing joint training sessions, workshops, and safety drills that involve both school personnel and community partners. This collaboration ensures a unified response in times of crisis and creates a lasting safety network. In building strong relationships with both parents and community organizations, schools create a holistic, resilient approach to safety that benefits every member of the educational ecosystem.

Notes

1. D. Osher et al., *Safe, Supportive and Successful Schools, Step by Step* (American Institutes for Research, 2004). https://www.prevention.org/Resources/46797fad-f5a7-4eac-9b7a-cc1edd920797/AIR_SafeSupportiveSuccessfulSchoolsStepbyStep.pdf.
2. J. de Niet et al., "Predictors of Participant Dropout at Various Stages of a Pediatric Lifestyle Program," *American Academy of Pediatrics*, January 1, 2011. https://doi.org/10.1542/peds.2010-0272.

3. National Association of School Psychologists, "School Safety and Crisis Resources," 2018. https://www.nasponline.org/resources-and-publications/resources-and-podcasts/school-safety-and-crisis.

4. U.S. Secret Service and U.S. Department of Education, "Safe School Initiative: An Interim Report on the Prevention of Targeted Violence in Schools," 2002. https://ojp.gov/ncjrs/virtual-library/abstracts/safe-school-initiative-interim-report-prevention-targeted-violence.

5. U.S. Department of Education, "Practical Information on Crisis Planning: A Guide for Schools and Communities," 2019.

6. R. Benbenishty and R. A. Astor, "Conceptual Foundations and Ecological Influences of School Violence, Bullying, and Safety," *American Psychological Association*, 2019. https://doi.org/10.1037/0000106-002.

7. D. L. Espelage and S. M. Swearer, eds. *Bullying in American Schools: A Social-Ecological Perspective on Prevention and Intervention* (Lawrence Erlbaum Associates, 2004).

8. V. P. Poteat and D. L. Espelage, "Predicting Psychosocial Consequences of Homophobic Victimization in Middle School Students," *The Journal of Early Adolescence*, 2007.

9. National Center for Safe Supportive Learning Environments, "Comprehensive School Safety," 2020.

10. U.S. Department of Education, "Practical Information on Crisis Planning: A Guide for Schools and Communities," 2019.

11. American School Counselor Association, "Ethical Standards for School Counselors," 2020. https://www.schoolcounselor.org/About-School-Counseling/Ethical-Responsibilities/ASCA-Ethical-Standards-for-School-Counselors-(1).

12. Emily Goodman-Scott, Christopher A. Sink, Blaire E. Cholewa, and Melanie Burgess, "An Ecological View of School Counselor Ratios and Student Academic Outcomes: A National Investigation," *Journal of Counseling and Development*, September 11, 2018. https://onlinelibrary.wiley.com/doi/10.1002/jcad.12221.

13. S. E. Brock et al., *School Crisis Prevention and Intervention: The PREPaRE Model*, 2nd ed. (National Association of School Psychologists, 2019).

14. G. T. Eells et al., *Crisis Prevention, Intervention, and Response: A Complete Guide for Schools*, 3rd ed. (Routledge, 2020).

15. Substance Abuse and Mental Health Services Administration, "SAMHSA's Concept of Trauma and Guidance for a Trauma-Informed Approach," 2014.

16. A. Goddard, "Adverse Childhood Experiences and Trauma-Informed Care," *National Library of Medicine*, October 28, 2020. https://pubmed.ncbi.nlm.nih.gov/33129624/.

17. Goodman-Scott et al., "An Ecological View of School Counselor Ratios and Student Academic Outcomes."

18. P. A. Wyman et al., "An Outcome Evaluation of the Sources of Strength Suicide Prevention Program Delivered by Adolescent Peer Leaders in High Schools," *American Journal of Public Health*, 2010. https://pubmed.ncbi.nlm.nih.gov/20634440/.

19. C. Zenner et al., "Mindfulness-based Interventions in Schools—A Systematic Review and Meta-analysis," *Frontiers in Psychology*, June 2014. https://www.researchgate.net/publication/264393931_Mindfulness-based_interventions_in_schools-a_systematic_review_and_meta-analysis.

20. N. S. Tobler, M. R. Roona, P. Ochshorn, D. G. Marshall, A. V. Streke, and K. M. Stackpole, "School-based Adolescent Drug Prevention Programs: 1998 Meta-analysis," *Journal of Primary Prevention*, 2000. https://psycnet.apa.org/record/2000-03397-002.

21. R. Borum, D. G. Cornell, W. Modzeleski, and S. R. Jimerson, "What Can Be Done About School Shootings? A Review of the Evidence," *Educational Researcher*, 2010. https://www.jstor.org/stable/27764551.

22. National School Public Relations Association, "Creating Effective School Communications During Crisis," 2020. https://www.nspra.org/PR-Resources/Samples-and-Resources-Gold-Mine.

23. National Association of School Resource Officers, "Standards and Best Practices for School Resource Officer Programs (4th ed.)," 2021. https://www.nasro.org/membership/resources-and-best-practices/.

24. U.S. Department of Education, "Practical Information on Crisis Planning: A Guide for Schools and Communities," 2018.

25. Eric Lesneskie and Stephen Block, "School Violence: The Role of Parental and Community Involvement," *Journal of School Violence*, 26 May 2016. https://doi.org/10.1080/15388220.2016.1168744.

Bibliography

American School Counselor Association. "Ethical Standards for School Counselors," 2022. https://www.schoolcounselor.org/About-School-Counseling/Ethical-Responsibilities/ASCA-Ethical-Standards-for-School-Counselors-(1).

Benbenishty, R., and R. A. Astor. "Conceptual Foundations and Ecological Influences of School Violence, Bullying, and Safety." *American Psychological Association*, 2019. https://doi.org/10.1037/0000106-002.

Borum, R., D. G. Cornell, W. Modzeleski, and S. R. Jimerson. "What Can Be Done About School Shootings? A Review of the Evidence." *Educational Researcher*, 2010. https://www.jstor.org/stable/27764551.

Brock, S. E., A. B. Nickerson, M. A. Reeves, S. R. Jimerson, R. A. Lieberman, and T. A. Feinberg. *School Crisis Prevention and Intervention: The PREPaRE Model*. 2nd ed. National Association of School Psychologists, 2019. https://iweb.nasponline.org/iweb/Purchase/ProductDetail.aspx?Product_code=N1618E.

Collaborative for Academic, Social, and Emotional Learning. "CASEL Guide: Effective Social and Emotional Learning Programs—Preschool and Elementary School Edition," 2021. https://pg.casel.org/.

Community Anti-Drug Coalitions of America. 2021. https://www.cadca.org.

Cornell, D., and M. J. Mayer. "Why Do School Order Codes Matter? The Influence of Order Codes on the Use of Exclusionary Discipline and Student Behavior." *Journal of Law and Education*, 2010. https://journals.sagepub.com/doi/abs/10.3102/0013189x09357616.

de Niet, J., M. Jongejan, J. Passchier, and E. van den Akker. "Predictors of Participant Dropout at Various Stages of a Pediatric Lifestyle Program." *American Academy of Pediatrics*, January 1, 2011. https://doi.org/10.1542/peds.2010-0272.

Dusenbury, L., J. Newman, R. P. Weissberg, P. Goren, C. Domitrovich, and A. Mart. "State Standards to Advance Social and Emotional Learning: Findings from CASEL's State Scan of Social and Emotional Learning Standards, Preschool Through High School," 2014. https://www.academia.edu/111781831/State_Standards_to_Advance_Social_and_Emotional_Learning_Findings_from_CASELs_State_Scan_of_Social_and_Emotional_Learning_Standards_Preschool_through_High_School_2014.

Dusenbury, L., R. P. Weissberg, P. Goren, and C. E. Domitrovich. "Development and Implementation of Standards for Social and Emotional Learning in the 50 States: A Brief on Findings from CASEL's Experience," 2016. https://www.academia.edu/91277472/Development_and_Implementation_of_Standards_for_Social_and_Emotional_Learning_in_the_50_States_A_Brief_on_Findings_from_CASELs_Experience.

Espelage, D. L., and S. M. Swearer, eds., *Bullying in American Schools: A Social-ecological Perspective on Prevention and Intervention*. Lawrence Erlbaum Associates, 2004. https://psycnet.apa.org/record/2004-00070-000.

Garcia, A., G. Sprang, and T. Clemans. "The Role of School Leaders in Cultivating a Trauma-Informed School Climate." *Children and Youth Services Review*, March 2023. https://doi.org/10.1016/j.childyouth.2023.106816.

Goddard, A. "Adverse Childhood Experiences and Trauma-Informed Care." *National Library of Medicine*, October 28, 2020. https://pubmed.ncbi.nlm.nih.gov/33129624/.

Goodman-Scott, E., C. A. Sink, B. E. Cholewa, and M. Burgess. "An Ecological View of School Counselor Ratios and Student Academic Outcomes: A National Investigation." *Journal of Counseling and Development*, September 11, 2018. https://onlinelibrary.wiley.com/doi/10.1002/jcad.12221.

Lesneskie, Eric, and Steven Block. "School Violence: The Role of Parental and Community Involvement." *Journal of School Violence*, May 26, 2016. https://doi.org/10.1080/15388220.2016.1168744.

National Association of School Psychologists. "School Safety and Crisis Resources." Accessed January 26, 2025. https://www.nasponline.org/resources-and-publications/resources-and-podcasts/school-safety-and-crisis.

National Association of School Resource Officers. "Standards and Best Practices for School Resource Officer Programs." (4th ed.). Accessed January 26,2025. https://www.nasro.org/membership/resources-and-best-practices/.

National Center for Safe Supportive Learning Environments. "Emotional Safety." Accessed January 26, 2025. https://safesupportivelearning.ed.gov/topic-research/safety/emotional-safety.

National School Public Relations Association. "Crisis and Safety Communication." Accessed January 26, 2025. https://www.nspra.org/PR-Resources/Samples-and-Resources-Gold-Mine.

Osher, D., K. Dwyer, and S. Jackson. *Safe, Supportive and Successful Schools, Step by Step*. American Institutes for Research, 2004. https://www.prevention.org/Resources/46797fad-f5a7-4eac-9b7a-cc1eda920797/AIR_SafeSupportiveSuccessfulSchoolsStepbyStep.pdf.

Poteat, V. P., and D. L. Espelage. "Predicting Psychosocial Consequences of Homophobic Victimization in Middle School Students." *The Journal of Early Adolescence*, 2007. https://journals.sagepub.com/doi/10.1177/0272431606294839.

Ramiro-Gonzalez, M., D. Dobermann, D. Metilka, E. Aldridge, Y. Yon, and D. Sethi. "Child Maltreatment Prevention: A Content Analysis of European National Policies." *National Library of Medicine*, February 1, 2019. https://pubmed.ncbi.nlm.nih.gov/30184076/.

Sandoval, Jonathan, ed. *Crisis Counseling, Intervention and Prevention In the Schools*. 3rd ed. 2013. https://www.routledge.com/Crisis-Counseling-Intervention-and-Prevention-in-the-Schools/Sandoval/p/book/9780415807715?srsltid=AfmBOooTz6R2dwaOpEhTfYl35C8pvXaPTDr470niMWObLxUzCQuabkyR.

Substance Abuse and Mental Health Services Administration. "SAMHSA's Concept of Trauma and Guidance for a Trauma-Informed Approach," 2014. https://ncsacw.acf.hhs.gov/userfiles/files/SAMHSA_Trauma.pdf.

Tobler, N. S., M. R. Roona, P. Ochshorn, D. G. Marshall, A. V. Streke, and K. M. Stackpole. "School-based Adolescent Drug Prevention Programs: 1998 Meta-analysis." *Journal of Primary Prevention*, 2000. https://psycnet.apa.org/record/2000-03397-002.

U.S. Department of Education. "Guide to the Individualized Education Program," 2000. https://www.ed.gov/sites/ed/files/parents/needs/speced/iepguide/iepguide.pdf.

U.S. Department of Education. "Practical Information on Crisis Planning: A Guide for Schools and Communities," January 2007. https://www.ed.gov/sites/ed/files/admins/lead/safety/emergencyplan/crisisplanning.pdf.

U.S. Secret Service and U.S. Department of Education. "Safe School Initiative: An Interim Report on the Prevention of Targeted Violence in Schools," 2000. https://ojp.gov/ncjrs/virtual-library/abstracts/safe-school-initiative-interim-report-prevention-targeted-violence.

Wyman, P. A., C. H. Brown, M. LoMurray, K. Schmeelk-Cone, M. Petrova, Q. Yu, and W. Wang. "An Outcome Evaluation of the Sources of Strength Suicide Prevention Program Delivered by Adolescent Peer Leaders in High Schools." *American Journal of Public Health*, 2010. https://pubmed.ncbi.nlm.nih.gov/20634440/.

Zenner, C., S. Herrnleben-Kurz, and H. Walach. "Mindfulness-based Interventions in Schools—A Systematic Review and Meta-analysis." *Frontiers in Psychology*, June 2014. https://www.researchgate.net/publication/264393931_Mindfulness-based_interventions_in_schools-a_systematic_review_and_meta-analysis.

4 Training for Emergencies

Training for emergencies is complex. There are five basic concepts that specifically apply to emergency training:

- Knowledge
- Preparedness
- Awareness
- Confidence
- Decisiveness

These terms combine into four basic educational tenets that are extremely important to framing training to prepare to successfully navigate emergencies:

- Knowledge enables Preparedness.
- Preparedness encourages Awareness.
- Preparedness and Awareness build Confidence.
- Confidence enables Decisiveness.

Each of these tenets builds upon the previous and are all key to being prepared to respond to emergencies. In addition, flexibility, improvisation, and managing emotions are also key concepts that all apply to emergency management.

Your Own Personal Emergency Example

A good way to relate to the criticality of training and preparing for emergencies can be found in this simple example. Think back to the first time you were involved in a serious traffic crash. It doesn't matter whether you were the driver or simply along for the ride. Think about how you would have answered these ten questions at that time:

1. Was it unexpected?
2. Did you immediately recognize what had happened?

3. Did you understand what immediate actions were necessary?
4. If there were injuries, did you know how to identify the most serious injuries, and prioritize what emergency medical actions were necessary?
5. Did you have any resources in the vehicles, such as first aid or other emergency gear?
6. Were the vehicles and passengers still in harm's way after the accident had occurred?
7. Did you immediately know what information needed to be relayed to first responders?
8. Did you know what the exact location was where the accident occurred?
9. Did you feel confident that you knew what to do, and were you able to manage your emotions when taking those actions?
10. Were you hurt, scared, anxious, angry, or upset?

> Quick Tip: Specific to the need for training to properly respond to critical incidents, the author of the book *Stay Safe*, and retired FBI Special Agent and Hostage Rescue Team operator Greg Shaffer says, "*The body cannot go where the mind has never been.*"

Emergency Management Training Terminology

A little terminology is important. There are some types of training exercises that are familiar to the school environment, but there is a spectrum of other types of training exercises related to emergency management that is important to understand.

Understanding these other types of training exercises and where they fit in will help make discussions with first responders and other public safety entities much more effective.

Along with learning and understanding the terminology that public safety utilities, it is also important to understand the specific training terminology for training that is applicable to your state's educational code. Depending on what state your school is in, there may be subtle but significant differences in the formal definitions of terms such as "drills" or "exercises."

Educating your local public safety partners on these distinctions to ensure clear communication is a great step forward toward communicating effectively.

The two main distinctions between types of exercises are discussion-based exercises and operations-based exercises.

Discussion-based exercises: These are used to familiarize participants with current plans, policies, and procedures, or may be used in the development of new plans. Discussion-based exercises have a spectrum of their own, ranging from a simple five-minute discussion at a staff meeting about an incident to a more complex tabletop exercise involving multiple agencies as participants in the discussion.

Tabletop Exercises involve key personnel discussing realistic but hypothetical scenarios in an informal and stress-free environment. This form of exercise can be used to assess current plans, procedures, or systems and help identify strengths and areas needing improvement.

Tabletop exercises typically bring together representatives from multiple agencies that would likely be responding to manage an emergency situation. No operational assets are deployed, and the notional response is simply discussed by the participants at the table.

Tabletop exercises are designed to identify friction points in response protocols, procedures, or resources. Tabletop exercises are a great way to build relationships with the leadership of your public safety agency partners. Learning how these exercises are facilitated is a great training opportunity to learn how to facilitate less complex tabletop exercises with school or district staff.

Tabletop exercises are typically two to three hours in duration. Participants will discuss two to three different notional scenarios. These exercises are facilitated by a trained facilitator who will guide the discussion. Exercise participants are known as players. It is also appropriate to invite staff who will likely participate in future exercises to participate simply as observers of the discussion.

Operations-Based Exercises: These are characterized by an actual reaction to a simulated scenario, including a response to emergency conditions, with mobilization of apparatus, resources, and commitment of personnel.

> Quick Tip: When planning any operations-based exercise that is likely to bring emergency vehicles to campus, it is important to ensure coordination with district and public safety public information officers. Multiple emergency vehicles on campus will absolutely be noticed by parents or the public, and it will be commented about on social media. This can easily be managed with a proactive statement from a public information officer regarding a training activity scheduled on campus.

- Drills are coordinated, supervised exercise activities that are normally used to test a specific operation or function. Schools commonly conduct fire evacuation drills, but a comprehensive approach to emergency management also requires practicing other procedures (shelter-in-place, lockdown, etc.) under a variety of conditions. This is the simplest type of operational exercise.
- Functional Exercises are like drills but involve multiple partners. These types of exercises are conducted in a realistic environment without movement of personnel and equipment. They are designed to test a specific function of the response, whether it's communication, standing up a command post, or many other different singular elements. Functional exercises are typically centered around communications and communications resources.
- Full-Scale Exercises are the most complex type of exercise. They are multiagency, multi-jurisdictional, multi-organizational exercises that validate many facets of preparedness. Full-scale exercises are conducted in real-time, creating a stressful, time-constrained environment that closely mirrors real events.

A Building Block Approach

Much like training school and district staff for emergencies, first responders also utilize a building block methodology—starting out with simpler training exercises, then gradually building in exercise complexity and resources deployed.

> Quick Tip: A great way to learn more about planning a successful training exercise is to participate as an observer or otherwise assist with a training exercise at another location before hosting your own. This gives great insight into what makes for a great, or perhaps not so great, training event.

Tabletop exercises and functional exercises are typically part of an exercise series culminating in a full-scale or FSE. Full-scale exercises involve the movement and positioning of emergency vehicles, establishing an incident command post, and coordinating physical response actions to the incident.

Full-scale exercises involve multiple responding agencies, who will come together to establish what is called unified command, where multiple agencies work together in a coordinated response. Depending on the goals and objectives of the exercise that are established in advance, the exercise may involve role players, simulating victims or aggressors, moulage or other injury simulation tools, props, and other resources designed to provide a realistic training experience for the first responders.

Planning for full-scale exercises is often the result of months of planning by an exercise design team, bringing agencies together to exercise the response to an incident. Full-scale exercises often have a very large and twofold purpose—one is to practice the coordination and communication between the management of an incident through unified command, and the second purpose is to give line responders the ability to train together. In an active shooter exercise, for example, police and fire agencies may work together to deploy a Rescue Task Force, a type of response where teams move throughout a school or other location, practicing actual incident response and tactical response skills.

The Incident Command System (ICS)

The Incident Command System was created as a way to manage large emergencies. ICS was originally developed in California many years ago to better manage wildfire responses, which often went far beyond a single-agency response. The ICS framework is currently used throughout the country at federal, state, and local levels.[1]

Understanding the basics of the Incident Command System (ICS) is important for school and district administrators who will have roles working with public safety agencies in the management of critical incidents.

There are five major management functions that comprise the ICS organizational structure.

Incident Command: The Incident Commander (IC) sets the incident objectives, strategies, and priorities and has overall responsibility for the incident. The incident commander is responsible for three things:

- Ensuring incident safety.
- Providing information and services to internal and external stakeholders.
- Establishing and maintaining liaison with other agencies participating in the incident.

The incident commander is the only position that is always staffed in ICS. In small incidents, the incident commander may accomplish all management functions. In a school, the incident commander is typically either the principal or assistant principal.

Operations: Performs operations to reach the defined incident objectives. Establishes operational tactics and directs all operational resources.

Planning: Supports the incident by tracking resources, collecting and analyzing information, and maintaining incident documentation.

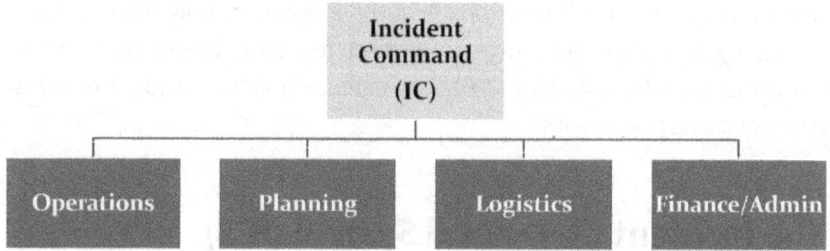

Figure 4.1. Basic Incident Command System (ICS) Structure. Glenn G. Norling www.trainbeready.com

STEM School Highlands Ranch, Highlands Ranch, Colorado

On May 7, 2019, at approximately 1:50 p.m., an identified student, 18, armed with a rifle and a handgun, and a second identified student, 16, armed with two handguns, allegedly began shooting in two different locations at the STEM School Highlands Ranch. After one student was killed during a confrontation with the first shooter, two other students subdued and disarmed the shooter, thereby ending the threat posed by that shooter. The second shooter wounded six students before being detained and disarmed by a private security officer.

www.fbi.gov

Figure 4.2. STEM School Highlands Ranch, Colorado. www.fbi.gov

Logistics: Provides resources and other needed services to support the incident objectives.

Finance and Administration: Tracks incident costs and provides accounting, procurement, financial documentation, and analysis.

These functions all apply whether the school is managing a routine emergency, preparing for a major nonemergency event, or managing the school's response to a disaster event. Depending on the complexity of the event, one person may fulfill multiple roles.

FEMA Emergency Management Institute

The Federal Emergency Management Agency (FEMA) Emergency Management Institute offers several free online independent study courses: https://training.fema.gov/is/ A FEMA SID number is required before registering for these courses. Obtain a FEMA SID number at https://cdp.dhs.gov/femasid/ by clicking on "Register for FEMA SID."[2]

ICS 100, Introduction to the Incident Command System, introduces the Incident Command System (ICS) and provides the foundation for higher-level ICS training. This course describes the history, features and principles, and organizational structure of the Incident Command System. It also explains the relationship between ICS and the National Incident Management System (NIMS). Target Audience: Persons involved with emergency planning, and response or recovery efforts.

ICS 200, the Basic Incident Command System for Initial Response, reviews the Incident Command System (ICS), provides the context for ICS within initial response, and supports higher-level ICS training. This course provides training on, and resources for, personnel who are likely to assume a supervisory position within ICS. Target Audience: Response personnel at the supervisory level who are involved with emergency planning, response, or recovery efforts.

FEMA's Emergency Management Institute has more than 200 emergency management courses, both online via their independent study program and in-person at locations around the country or at FEMA's primary training facility in Alabama.

Maximizing Training Value

Here are six basic principles to help maximize training value for staff:

- Train all staff specifically in the school/district safety plan procedures and processes. Ensure all staff members have access to and are familiar with the safety plan. Recognize that transitory, transfer, or part-time employees may not have been present during your development training at the beginning of the school year.
- Incorporate safety and incident response into everyday topics and discussions with staff and students as much as possible.
- When lockdown drills are conducted, invite public safety personnel to participate.
- If the school/district staff has emergency response resources on campus, such as Stop the Bleed kits, purchase training versions of the same equipment that staff can train with.
- Continuously seek out additional training opportunities for staff.
- Safety and emergency training should be conducted continuously throughout the year. Establishing a training roadmap is key and is discussed in detail later in this chapter.

Plan? What Plan?

A key point about school and district emergency plans is that administrators are often more familiar with emergency plans than their staff are. It is very important to ensure that all staff have access to the plan, have reviewed it, have trained to it, and are familiar with the basic response principles in the plan.

This is especially true as plans are updated, when security technologies are deployed on campus, and when points of contact are changed.

A second key point is that temporary staff, such as substitute teachers, and most classified staff, do not typically receive training on, or even exposure to school emergency plans. A school or district can have the greatest safety plan put in place, but if staff, students, and faculty have never trained to it, it will not be effective when it is needed the most.[3]

> Quick Tip: Routine, tiny "touchpoints" matter. Normalize incorporating emergency response discussion into weekly staff meetings. Add a very short five-minute discussion about a simple emergency issue, or resource. The more emergency management concepts that staff are able to discuss in short, simple discussions help build a solid foundation for more complex situations. Keep it relevant to all by discussing issues staff will likely encounter throughout the school year.

"It's Not MY Problem!"

Emergencies often happen at the least convenient times, or when staff are least prepared. As the old saying goes, "Murphy" likes to show up when we least expect it.

If certain staff members are naysayers, or perhaps verbal opponents of emergency planning and training, try to place them in a position of responsibility. Have a discussion of an emergency situation that administrators would typically handle, except place these staff members in an acting role for the day, simulating the administrator being away from campus.

Succession planning is an important aspect of training staff, as many times, administrators or other key personnel are not on campus when something requires an immediate response.[4]

Taking the Next Step

There are always opportunities to take the next step as far as ensuring schools and districts are better prepared, better trained, and better equipped to handle and manage emergencies. If the basic topics covered previously are satisfactorily addressed. Here is a list of potential next steps, to continue with:

- Conduct a lockdown drill during a passing period, or immediately before or after school. Invite administrators from other school sites to help support the challenges of running lockdown drills during those times.

- Safety and security conferences are not just for the SRO. They can be very valuable to staff members, especially if they're a part of the school safety or school site safety committee.
- As a school or perhaps through the local parent-teacher organization, sponsor a Stop the Bleed class for your community. Partner with a local fire department or medical center/hospital.
- Take every opportunity to bring public safety personnel on campus and take every opportunity to invite them into classrooms. Invite them to school events and to meet with school safety committees or staff.
- Advocate for preparedness resources for your school site. If your school does not have trauma kits or Stop the Bleed kits on campus, partner with a local community organization to purchase them, and provide training for staff in their use.
- Invite police and fire agencies to train on campus when school is not in session. If there are available meeting rooms on campus, invite public safety agencies to host interagency meetings public safety meetings at the school.
- If you have an assigned School Resource Officer who has a vehicle assigned to them, consider adding a graphic of the school mascot to their official vehicle.
- School emergency planning does not start and stop with the school day. If the school has before or after-school programs, athletic events, or any other events outside of the school day. Ensure that safety and security planning and procedures are part of those events.[5]

Quick Tip: One very effective emergency preparedness aid that should be in every classroom is a laminated two-page (front and back) emergency quick reference sheet. It should have emergency contact numbers, scene safety directions, basic response protocols, quick medical advice, and very basic stress management tips. This simple reference card can help a staff member mentally re-center and gives them something to focus on in an emergency.

Leading from the Front

Training to prepare for and effectively respond to emergencies is important. Administrators must ensure that the importance of this training is not unintentionally minimized in front of staff or students.[6]

Lead from the front by taking exercises seriously, as the lifesaving trainings that they are, and ensure staff members do the same. These training exercises and drills take precious minutes away from classroom instruction time, which is challenging.

During lockdown and other drills, administrators set the tone. Teachers should not be allowed to close and lock their doors and blinds, turn lights off, and continue their block of instruction. This happens far too often, and truly minimizes the potential value of the training.

> Quick Tip: All staff should have a very clear understanding that when there is a situation on campus involving a life safety concern, that the singular focus for all involved staff at the time is successfully managing the incident, both for staff and students. Everything else is secondary.
>
> There is no better way to ensure that staff and students are prepared for an emergency than by providing as many training opportunities and realistic training events as feasible.

Develop a Training Roadmap

Developing a safety training roadmap for the school. Much like designing curriculum and scheduling school year activities such as assemblies, special events, and athletic events, start the school year by preparing an emergency management training roadmap that continues throughout the school calendar year.[7]

Why a Roadmap? Another Sports-Related Example Will Give You a Good Perspective

Consider a student sent to a weeklong national sports camp, headlined by a professional athlete, where they participate in all sorts of activities designed to test their skill levels and learn new skills. That same student does not participate in physical conditioning activities or play the sport at all during the following year and then returns to the same sports camp the next year.

Contrast that with another student who attends the first year's training camp, then conditions and trains all year long in that sport with practices, games, and tournaments, and then returns to the same sports camp a year later.

Which student will have likely grown in conditioning and sports skills? Will the first student even maintain their original level of a year ago? Emergency planning is the same way.

Schedule and conduct training events in a building block approach. Start with simple awareness discussions on the school safety plan and discuss specific emergency procedures and processes.

Bring public safety partners in to discuss issues and continue building that relationship throughout the year. See if they would be willing to plan a tabletop exercise, functional exercise, or full-scale exercise at the school.

Include athletic stadiums, fields, and other venues where special events are held on campus. This will require close coordination with the school athletic director and facilities staff.

> Quick Tip: Emergency planning and training can be like trying to hit a moving target. As district or school facilities are modified or new communications or security technology is implemented, it is important to ensure that all your staff understands the new facility, technology capability, or process. Sometimes you may need to step back to ensure that everybody has a solid baseline to utilize the new changes.

As with all planning activities, emergency management planning should be done in close coordination and collaboration with key staff members, who can also share in the planning workload. This training roadmap needs to fit in with all the other competing calendar activities across the school campus. It will likely require some level of approval at the district level also.

Safety and emergency planning should also include students, so look for every opportunity to incorporate student leadership into the process.

Bringing It Home: Are YOU prepared?

Emergencies have a way of finding the exact moments when we are least prepared, or least ready to deal with a critical incident. As a school administrator, it is important to make sure that you are prepared to respond to an incident anytime you are at the school.

You also need to be prepared to respond to a potential threat at any time—whether it is during the school day, in the evenings, overnight, or on weekends and holidays. Perhaps you have multiple administrative staff members who can rotate this responsibility outside of school hours. Potential threats also have the same penchant for arising at the least convenient moment.

Part of being prepared to respond to emergencies requires having a copy of the emergency plan available, ready access to emergency points of contact for the school, and access to staff and student information. Recognize that there may be times when electronic access to databases may not be available—whether on campus or via remote secure network login. So having a backup Plan B and Plan C is prudent. A little bit of planning goes a long way.

Training to Support Prevention

- A trained and active behavioral assessment team is a critical part of ensuring the safety of your staff and students.
- Staff, students, parents, and community members must be educated on concerning behaviors, encouraged to report them, and also clearly understand the methodology to report them.

As an administrator, you are a key school behavioral assessment team member. Having access to behavioral assessment team member's contact

> **Central Visual and Performing Arts High School, St. Louis, Missouri**
>
> On October 24, 2022, at approximately 9:11 a.m., an identified shooter, 19, armed with a rifle, began shooting at people at the Central Visual and Performing Arts High School. Two people were killed (one teacher and one student); seven people (students) were wounded. The shooter was killed by law enforcement after an exchange of gunfire at the scene.
>
> www.fbi.gov

Figure 4.3. Central Visual and Performing Arts High School, Missouri. www.fbi.gov

information, forms, and other documentation at any time is important. Ensure you understand exactly how to report concerning behavior and fully understand the assessment process.[8]

Current technology provides a host of robust reporting platforms that enable detailed reporting via telephone, mobile device, or online. Reporting concerning behavior is a key part of keeping the campus safe.

Encouraging the reporting of concerning or suspicious behavior, similar to encouraging and supporting reports of bullying, is important for staff, students, parents, and community members.

The Secret Sauce

- Integrate Planning and training for emergencies into your daily routine as much as possible—but ensure you are keeping a positive focus—not a doom and gloom attitude.
- Solicit feedback—as painful as that may be.
- After every critical incident and training event, an After Action Review (AAR) should be conducted to determine what worked, what didn't work, what needs to be fixed, and how the school could be better prepared for the next time.[9]
- Bring safety preparedness into the mainstream—it should be discussed with staff (all staff), students, parents, and community members.
- Engage with your community mental health resources to proactively train staff on resiliency, stress management, and critical decision-making in an emergency. Public safety agencies can be good resources for discussing emotional resiliency in the face of trauma.

> Quick Tip: Emergency preparedness training should be done with a keen eye on the emotions of staff and must be mindful of the potential emotional sensitivity surrounding preparing for critical incidents.

- We all have a role in school safety, and it is important to further that discussion so that everyone recognizes that they have a responsibility and a role—many people and most students do not.
- As challenging and as painful as emergency preparedness planning can be, there is no more burdensome cost than to be unable to answer the question: What do we do when "what if" becomes "what now?"

Notes

1. "School Incident Command System (ICS) Roles and Responsibilities," National Association of School Psychologists, accessed June 2, 2024, https://apps.nasponline.org/search-results.aspx?q=School+Incident+Command+System+%28ICS%29+Roles+and+Responsibilities.
2. "FEMA Exercise and Preparedness Tools," Federal Emergency Management Agency, accessed June 2, 2024, https://www.fema.gov/emergency-managers/national-preparedness/exercises/tools.
3. "Guide For Developing High-Quality School Emergency Operations Plans," Federal Emergency Management Agency, 2013, https://rems.ed.gov/docs/School_Guide_508C.pdf.
4. "Practical Information on Crisis Planning: A Guide for Schools and Communities," U.S. Department of Education, January 2007, http://www2.ed.gov/admins/lead/safety/emergencyplan/crisisplanning.pdf.
5. "Timeless School Safety Strategies," Readiness and Emergency Management for Schools Technical Assistance Center, accessed June 2, 2024, https://rems.ed.gov/docs/Timeless-Strategies-Fact-Sheet_508C.pdf.
6. John P. Jarvis and Brittany N. Murray, "Leadership During Crisis Response," *FBI Law Enforcement Bulletin*, May 8, 2019, https://leb.fbi.gov/articles/featured-articles/leadership-during-crisis-response-current-research.
7. "Ten Essential Actions to Improve School Safety," School Safety Working Group Report to the Attorney General, 2020, https://portal.cops.usdoj.gov/resourcecenter/content.ashx/cops-w0891-pub.pdf.
8. "Prior Knowledge of Potential School-Based Violence: Information Students Learn May Prevent a Targeted Attack," U.S. Secret Service, May 2008, https://www.secretservice.gov/node/2568.
9. "Final Report of the Federal Commission on School Safety," Federal Commission On School Safety, Presented to the President of the United States, December 18, 2018, https://www2.ed.gov/documents/school-safety/school-safety-report.pdf.

Bibliography

Federal Commission on School Safety. "Final Report of the Federal Commission on School Safety." Presented to the President of the United States, December 18, 2018. https://www2.ed.gov/documents/school-safety/school-safety-report.pdf.

Federal Emergency Management Agency. "FEMA Exercise and Preparedness Tools." Accessed June 2, 2024. https://www.fema.gov/emergency-managers/national-preparedness/exercises/tools.

Federal Emergency Management Agency. "Guide For Developing High-Quality School Emergency Operations Plans," 2013. https://rems.ed.gov/docs/School_Guide_508C.pdf.

Jarvis, John P., and Brittany N. Murray, "Leadership During Crisis Response." *FBI Law Enforcement Bulletin*, May 8, 2019. https://leb.fbi.gov/articles/featured-articles/leadership-during-crisis-response-current-research.

National Association of School Psychologists. "School Incident Command System (ICS) Roles and Responsibilities." Accessed June 2, 2024. https://apps.nasponline.org/search-results.aspx?q=School+Incident+Command+System+%28ICS%29+Roles+and+Responsibilities.

National Counterterrorism Center. "First Responder's Toolbox: Complex Operating Environment—Educational Facilities: Primary and Secondary Schools," June 29, 2019. https://www.dni.gov/files/NCTC/documents/jcat/firstresponderstoolbox/Complex_Operating_Environment_Education_Facilities_Primary_Secondary_Schools.pdf.

Readiness and Emergency Management for Schools Technical Assistance Center. REMS TA Center website. Accessed June 2, 2024. https://rems.ed.gov/.

Readiness and Emergency Management for Schools Technical Assistance Center. "Timeless School Safety Strategies." Accessed June 2, 2024. https://rems.ed.gov/docs/Timeless-Strategies-Fact-Sheet_508C.pdf.

School Safety Working Group Report to the Attorney General. "Ten Essential Actions to Improve School Safety," 2020. https://portal.cops.usdoj.gov/resourcecenter/content.ashx/cops-w0891-pub.pdf.

U.S. Department of Education. "Practical Information on Crisis Planning: A Guide for Schools and Communities," January 2007. http://www2.ed.gov/admins/lead/safety/emergencyplan/crisisplanning.pdf.

U.S. Secret Service. "Prior Knowledge of Potential School-Based Violence: Information Students Learn May Prevent a Targeted Attack," May 2008. https://www.secretservice.gov/node/2568.

5 Communications in Crisis

Good communication is the bridge between confusion and clarity.
—Nat Turner

Clear, calm, concise, and timely. It sounds so simple. Yet we have struggled from the very beginning with communicating effectively. Communication is just as much an art as it is a science.[1]

Beyond these four simple tenets of communication, we have to strive to minimize the impact of our emotions, the effects of the crisis itself, the crushing pressure of the situation, and the experience or inexperience of the administrator.

The school administrator has a critical and pivotal role in ensuring effective communication in a crisis. The ability to communicate swiftly and effectively during a critical incident is vital to a successful response and is often rooted in the preparations that have taken place beforehand.[2]

Administrators who have taken the time to prioritize and establish communications protocols and policies, participate in and conduct training, and—key to success in communicating during a crisis—establish trusted relationships before a critical event have a much higher chance of success.

This chapter will focus on three key areas: Communication preparations for a crisis, communication during a crisis, and, quite naturally, communication after a crisis. Key concepts and specific problem areas to focus on will be discussed, and quick reference guides for each will also be provided at the end of this book.

It Will Never Happen Here, Right? Preparing for a Crisis

Consider the Audience

When creating and establishing crisis communications plans in advance, it is essential to consider the information needs of the various audiences who desire or need information. What are these different audiences? They could be staff, students, parents, school board members, management, government officials. Also, another key audience is the public, and there is a distinction between the affected public and the unaffected public to consider. When determining the information needs of each of these audiences, recognizing that their needs are different is essential to creating a comprehensive crisis communications plan. The next step is to build plans to ensure consistent messaging across all communications platforms and to all stakeholders.[3]

Essential Elements of an Effective Communication Strategy

When designing an effective communications strategy, there are three primary points to consider:

One—Always plan ahead.

Two—Plan the method (platform or platforms) to acknowledge a crisis situation as soon as possible. Having information regarding the precise details of the crisis is not the purpose at this time. Advising of a crisis as quickly as possible establishes that the incident is being managed and does not overwhelm the leadership. It is appropriate at this point in time to say "we don't know yet" when pressed for details.

Three—It is critical to always tell the truth. Never try to control a narrative or engage in any kind of damage control. The message always has to be the truth, and this is often referred to as being "responsibly transparent."[4]

Relationships and Trust

Perhaps the most effective strategy to improve communication during a critical incident is to build public trust long before the crisis occurs.[5] In virtually every crisis situation, new partnerships, new team members, and new agencies are brought together in a stressful situation. Establishing partnerships and building rapport as much as possible before an incident occurs is extremely important. Why is this so important? In managing a crisis, not only does communication matter, but these partners require trust and confidence in their partners to be able to work together effectively. Building rapport and a trusted relationship during a crisis is exceedingly difficult.[6]

> Quick Tip: Trust requires hard and consistent work to establish. One small "white lie" can erode months of effort to build trust in a single moment. Rebuilding trust is exceedingly more difficult to accomplish.

Effective communication trust between the communicator and the audience(s), audience involvement, and emotional responses to risk. Communication is especially challenging as the spectrum of media platforms has changed the landscape significantly. This is true for both the communicator and the audience.[7]

Conduct a Communications Inventory

In order to establish a clear baseline, conduct a communications inventory. Determine your primary, secondary, and even tertiary communication methods. Start with your landline telephone system and understand what capabilities it has in terms of crisis communications.

Does your school utilize two-way radios? You should be able to answer questions such as: How are they used, who has access to them, where are they positioned, and who has access to the channels to monitor them?

Do you utilize district-issued cell phones or connect with teachers through their personal cell phones?

Starting with an inventory of all the different communication methods, you can build an effective training protocol to integrate communications during drills and other training events for the school.

Specific to two-way radios, it's important for you to understand the capabilities of local law enforcement and fire two-way radio systems in your facilities. Many schools are constructed such that public safety radio systems often have trouble reaching through their brick and cement walls. Understand where the communication challenges are in your school and try to resolve them with your public safety partners.[8]

Routine versus Emergency Operations

All too often, emergency communications systems are not utilized routinely. This causes anxiety and confusion when we need these systems in an emergency because staff are not familiar with them. As part of a communications training plan, building in some type of routine use for these systems daily or weekly is a huge benefit when the system is needed in a crisis.

A Spectrum of Communication

Emergency response plans must establish primary and secondary methods of communication among school staff, security personnel, first responders, and other key stakeholders. Depending on the nature of the crisis, communications infrastructure may become compromised during an event. Crisis incidents may also require communication among federal, state, local, and even private sector stakeholders. Many of these entities may have different communications capabilities, which need preplanning to ensure interoperability. Effective real-time communication using multiple platforms can ensure a common message and potentially reduce confusion and requests for information.[9]

Understand what methods are in place for communicating with staff, students, families, and the media. Start with planning the communication process to notify students and staff about an incident and instruct them on what to do.

The Common Word

A common vocabulary is necessary. School staff and emergency responders need to know each other's terminology. Work with emergency responders to develop a common vocabulary. The words used to give directions for evacuation, lockdown, and other actions should be clear and not hazard-specific. The Federal Emergency Management Agency recommends using plain language to announce the need for action, for example, "evacuate" rather than "code blue." Many schools have found that with plain language, everyone in the school building, including new staff, substitute teachers, and visitors, will understand the needed response.[10]

"This is the time to speak clearly and simply in order to prevent messages from being distorted, misunderstood, or worse yet, being transmitted factually incorrectly."[11]

Press Conference Preplanning

Successful press conferences require some preplanning. Schools and districts have to open channels of communication well before a crisis. Cultivate a relationship with city emergency managers, public works officials, health and mental health professionals, and the local media.[12]

The first preplanning task is to maintain a contact list of the public information officers from public safety agencies such as police, fire, emergency medical response, hospitals, local government officials, utility providers, and even large public venues in the area.

The next task is to pre-identify methods available for joint communications. These may be social media platforms, email rosters and lists, local government subscription notification systems, or systems such as reverse 911. Develop memorandums of understanding with surrounding agencies as needed and plan in advance to be able to use flexible and variable delivery methods in a crisis.

The final task to complete prior to a crisis is to compile a list of local media contact information and ensure you understand how to deliver press releases to the media.[13]

It's Time to Start Training

It is important to incorporate communication elements in training exercises. The building block approach to training exercises is very effective. Start with a simple five-minute discussion in a weekly staff meeting; then conduct a discussion-based exercise called a tabletop exercise where a notional scenario is presented, and the response is discussed by all participants. Next is a functional exercise where the primary purpose is to test a specific response to a scenario (communication in this case). These exercises build up to a full-scale exercise, where school and public safety personnel physically respond to a simulated crisis incident on campus with role players, props, and people simulating an active threat as well as injured students or faculty.

Internal Training

Simple training touch points regarding communications routinely have a huge value in providing familiarity with communication systems and emergency protocols and procedures.

Test communications equipment and methods during training and exercises together with local public safety agencies.[14]

Establish, maintain, test, and train on communication technology and protocols, such as emergency alerts, mass notifications, and intercom announcements, designed to alert staff and students, parents, and the local community.

External Training

Work with local public safety agencies to test, drill, and exercise the communications equipment the first responders will use during a response to ensure its adequacy. Often, the physical construction of school buildings can make radio or cell phone communication within the school buildings difficult.

Communication with local public safety agencies prior to emergencies to develop action plans and be part of training exercises is critical to making sure all resources are involved in the prevention and preparedness phase.[15]

When What If Becomes What Now? Communicating during a Crisis

"someone who demonstrates successful leadership in an office setting is not guaranteed to exhibit effective leadership when responding to a crisis—the opposite also holds true."[16]

Communication Challenges Are Nothing New

In his testimony before the Federal Commission on School Safety, Max Schachter, CEO and Founder of Safe Schools for Alex, observed that the interoperability of communications equipment, which was a problem during the 9/11 attacks, remains a problem today. He further testified that during the response to the Parkland shooting, a lack of interoperable equipment forced law enforcement to resort to hand signals.[17]

Communication: Is It Art or Science?

The answer, of course, is that it can be accurately characterized as both.

> Leaders must go beyond reviewing someone else's perspective of the subject's writing or statements. They need to invest the time in reading the literature themselves. Those leaders who apply leadership curiosity and seek out these writings can learn from them, develop an understanding of the type of incident they are facing, and prepare an appropriate course of action.[18]

Author Anthony Robbins put it this way: "To effectively communicate, we must realize that we're all different in the way we perceive the world and use this understanding as a guide to our communication with others." Communication challenges in a crisis situation are only exacerbated by psychological and mental barriers limiting the processing of information.[19]

In one crisis leadership study, interviewees stressed the "importance of training continuously and remaining a student of leadership." Seeking out and reading scholarly articles and case studies to actively participate in full-scale training exercises is very important. Education, along with experience, is essential for response readiness.[20]

The Action Imperative

What is the action imperative? In a crisis situation, there is continuous pressure to do something. Leaders all want to demonstrate that they are properly managing the crisis. Sometimes, the best action to take in a critical situation is to stop, take a deep breath, and focus on the situation. This

> **Gwinnett County School Bus, Suwanee, Georgia**
>
> On May 9, 2022, at approximately 7:15 a.m., an identified shooter, 57, armed with a gun, began shooting at people on a bus in a residential neighborhood. One person was wounded (bus driver, an employee). The shooter was apprehended by law enforcement at another location.
>
> www.fbi.gov

Figure 5.1. Gwinnett County School, Georgia. www.fbi.gov

enables leaders to take deliberate action rather than just doing "something." When the action imperative pushes leaders to demonstrate leadership by just doing something, it often creates more work, rather than carefully taking deliberate focused actions designed to solve the problems at hand.[21]

Managing Emotion and Stress

Leaders in law enforcement focus on "Mission first, people always." Personnel are a priority, especially in times of crisis. Have they eaten, slept, spoken with their families, or had a chance to share their ideas? To be an effective leader in crisis requires listening, soliciting feedback, seeking advice, and remaining approachable. This is one of the most vital characteristics that can foster positive outcomes both in and out of crisis response. It is also important to manage your own emotions and stress levels.[22]

Breathe Like a U.S. Navy SEAL

A stress management breathing technique commonly known as "Box Breathing" allows inhalation and exhalation to contribute to the balancing of acid/base in the blood. This is the simplest of all the breathing strategies and is useful for stress reduction. It is a form of yoga deep breathing used to help become and stay calm. The United States Navy SEALs have used box breathing for decades.

Its name refers to a box with four sides—a concept represented by breathing in while slowly counting to four, holding your breath while slowly counting to four, exhaling while slowly counting to four, and holding your breath while you slowly count to four after your exhale. This cycle is repeated four times.[23]

One Model Communication Approach

The Federal Bureau of Investigation's Behavioral Analysis Unit has developed a five-step communications model that can be applied to managing crisis communications down to a simple one-on-one discussion.[24]

This model is designed to be followed in order, as each previous step builds upon the previous one.

1. The first step is to employ active listening. Everyone thinks they know how to actively listen, but it really does take a significant amount of concentration and focus. Methodologies for active listening will be discussed later in this chapter.

2. The second step is to display empathy. Demonstrate understanding of the other's perspective. This is not agreeing with or condoning actions or behavior. It is simply demonstrating an understanding of where the other person is coming from.

3. The third step is to build rapport. This is trying to make a connection with the other person or persons. This is commonly referred to as "speaking their language."

4. The fourth step is to gradually exert your influence and attempt to help the other person move toward your perspective. Since rapport has been built, and active listening has allowed you to understand their perspective clearly, is it possible to create a common ground toward a solution?
5. The fifth step and final step is to initiate behavioral change. This is done by proposing a solution that now makes sense to the other person.

Three Simple Rules

Effective crisis communication starts with three simple rules:

Rule One: Plan Ahead.

Creating detailed contingency plans outlining every potential crisis and the appropriate response is time-consuming and painstaking, which is why many schools don't spend much effort on them. However, when faced with a crisis, these plans will save critical time and resources.

Rule Two: Speed Is Key.

Acknowledge crisis situations immediately. You may not have all of the details for days or weeks, but a prompt announcement to the media and your key stakeholders will minimize speculation and rumors and, most importantly, let them know you are in control.

Rule Three: Be Responsibly Transparent.

The truth will keep you free.
We're all familiar with the Enron, AIG, BP, and VW debacles; we've seen, time and again, how subterfuge and lies destroy organizations. These cases present powerful lessons in PR: Be up front. Take responsibility. Tell the truth. ever engage in cover-up, deceit, or unethical behavior of any kind. Remember that bad behavior will always find its way to the headlines—eventually.[25]

Manage the Media—Don't Let Them Manage You

There are a few simple ways to avoid becoming overwhelmed by the media. The first is to predesignate additional staff members to assist in managing the media. This is key to supporting leaders by allowing them to do what they need to do, and that is leading the incident response. The second thing to determine as quickly as possible is to determine what information can be released in the first minutes. Work on getting that message out quickly—even if it's a very short message. The key is to get something out quickly. Next is to get all the public information officers from each agency involved speaking together, so that the response going through the incident commander can be coordinated and is consistent across all agencies.

Finally, ensure any media messaging is done in coordination with the incident unified command, which will likely involve the school district, fire, and police at a minimum.[26] Designate a Public Information Officer (PIO) to establish contact with the media and to consistently provide appropriate information. Work with the incident command and the PIO(s) to control media access to and distance from, the event, crime scene, first responders and other public safety personnel, victims, and family members. Designate a specific area for press that does not interfere with first-responder or incident command operations.

Provide the media with information on all communication platforms (toll-free numbers, websites, social media, community information systems, etc.) used to deliver public updates and other relevant information.[27]

Surviving the Press Conference

A very popular local leader spoke publicly very often, back in the 1970s. He had a small wooden desktop lectern he used to travel with. On the speaker's side of the podium, at the top of the podium, clearly visible only to the speaker it said:

> "Stand Up. Speak Up. Shut Up. Sit Down."

Consider the simplicity of this instruction and apply to your own time at the podium.

Eleven keys to speaking effectively, whether at a press conference or in a private interview are:

- Words have consequences. Use the right words.
- Don't babble. Know what to say. Say it, and then repeat it.

- If you don't know the answer, stop talking.
- Focus on informing the audience. Use common and clear language.
- Expect everything you say to appear in print or electronic media.
- Never lie.
- Don't make promises you can't keep.
- Avoid using no comment. Explain why you can't answer.
- Saying "I don't know" is an acceptable response and can actually build credibility. Immediately follow the "I don't know" with a statement that explains why you don't know (e.g., early in the investigation) and when and how you will provide further information to answer the questions.[28]
- Don't argue or lose your cool. Media will always win in that situation.
- Don't speculate, guess intent, or accept assumptions.[29]

Guidelines for Working with the Media

- Be prepared. Be honest. Be brief. Be accessible.
- Understand all the facts, especially technical ones, and stick to them.
- Keep cool. Do not become defensive; do not lose your temper or argue.
- Develop a written statement to be read and handed out.
- Determine where members of the media can gather in case of a major emergency.
- This will likely be off campus, but ideally within view of the school.
- Stress concern for student safety and positive actions taken by the school or district.
- Do not make statements about responsibility until all the facts are known.
- Pause and collect your thoughts before you respond to reporters' questions.
- The interview is not over until the reporter leaves. Always be careful about what you say in the presence of a reporter before or after an interview. The microphone may still be on.

- Do not respond to negative questions by repeating words that inflame the situation: "Yes, it is a real tragedy that ..."
- Be alert to statements that begin with: Is it true that ... ? Are you really saying that ... ? How do you respond to ... ? Are you aware that ... ?
- Avoid "what if" questions. You cannot predict the future.
- Do not say, "No comment." Instead, try "I will have to check into the matter. What is your deadline? I will get back to you."
- Do not speak "off the record." The cost can be too high if that agreement is not respected.
- Avoid using educational terminology or acronyms.
- Know what is being done to help staff and students manage the situation. (NSPRA, 2016)
- Social Media. Words Matter!

Communication using a variety of platforms from internal messaging systems, media outlets, Meta, X (formerly Twitter) and other forms of social media can be a great benefit before, during, and after a school critical incident.[30]

Social media platforms such as X, Facebook, and Instagram offer a swift and cost-effective way to communicate to a large, diverse, and increasingly connected population. Five years ago, in 2018, 89 percent of Americans were current internet users, and in 2019, 73 percent of U.S. adults used social media, according to the Pew Research Center and Perrin & Anderson.[31]

Social Media Infrastructure Advantages

One significant benefit that social media platforms potentially bring to communications in crisis is on the event of a large, weather-related or other catastrophic event, such as an earthquake. These events are characterized by extensive impacts to infrastructure, such as no electricity, no cell phone service, 911 call centers becoming overwhelmed, and transportation all but halted. Social media can be a method to get critical information out when standard communications platforms are not available, not working, or otherwise compromised.

Social media can also be used internally, communicating with team members, rather than using traditional internal communications networks.[32]

Leaders managing a crisis can capitalize on social media's potential to create dialogue and proactively choose the right message and the best timing. This requires having a social media plan in place before a crisis occurs and integrating social media communications into an overall crisis communications strategy.[33]

Participation Trophies

The integrated use of social media platforms tremendously increases the ability for a continuous sharing of information in these ways:

- They are participatory communication platforms.
- They can generate, replicate, and sustain multi-way communication.
- They give agencies the opportunity to communicate with the public in real time and also in an authentic manner.
- They have transformed crisis communication from a one-way, linear approach to a continuous exchange and flow of information between those managing the crisis and the public.
- The "push and pull" of information and ideas through questions, concerns, and sharing of opinions gives officials an opportunity to respond.
- Agencies can engage in real-time conversations, respond to questions and concerns, and correct misinformation and rumors.[34]

Don't Be Tone-Deaf

One particular aspect of communicating through social media platforms that must be considered is tone. It is very important to focus on expressing empathy, sincerity, and building rapport thought social media. It is very easy to misunderstand communications that are limited in scope and approach. Sarcasm, for example, does not translate well through social media platforms, especially in a crisis situation. Social media platforms can be a very effective tool as part of a crisis communications strategy. Posts and other information disseminated should be considered as carefully as a written press release.[35]

> **Robb Elementary School, Uvalde, Texas**
>
> On May 24, 2022, at approximately 11:32 a.m., an identified shooter, 18, armed with a rifle, began shooting at people at Robb Elementary School. Twenty-one people were killed (19 students, two teachers); 17 people were wounded (including three law enforcement officers). The shooter was killed by law enforcement after an exchange of gunfire at the scene.
>
> www.fbi.gov

Figure 5.2. Robb Elementary School, Texas. www.fbi.gov

Social Media Posting Guidelines

- Make sure all social media content and activities have gone through the agency's internal clearance and approval process.
- Use direct and clear language to minimize or eliminate misinterpreting information. Be honest and accurate.
- Use images and videos cautiously. Ensure images and videos help convey the information you are trying to disseminate, and always verify they are not explicit or controversial.

- Be cautious of what links are included in posts. Always fact-check online sources to ensure they are credible, accurate, and help support and advance key messages.
- Be timely. Social media updates happen in real time. Release information when it is still relevant and constantly refresh information. Waiting too long to release posts suggests hiding something, or that the agency is incompetent, or lacks control of the situation.
- Correctly address misinformation and rumors. Rather than responding directly to someone posting false information, focus on the issue, and not the person with a post that addresses the issue directly, eliminating the likelihood of a counterattack.
- Review, review, and review again! The internet is forever: Even if you can delete a post, people are able to screenshot and save posts that may have misleading or inaccurate information. In your review, ensure the post is accurate, appropriate, and all grammar and spelling are correct.[36]

Technology Is Not Always Our Friend

One key point that leaders who have experienced critical situations have discussed is the failure of communications technology as a common issue during a crisis incident. This is especially common in rural areas where there is significant distance or geography across the large area, or during significant weather events. Some of the challenges have been:

- Poor cell phone or mobile service, or the overwhelming of networks due to call volume.
- Different radio frequencies between neighboring public safety agencies.
- A lack of equipment that is interoperable between agencies.
- A lack of knowledge about information management systems used by partner agencies.

Having alternative plans for when technology is not working is key to preparing for an emergency. The availability of dry erase boards or large paper pads and markers that can quickly step in to serve when technology is not available is a priority backup plan.[37]

It's Not Over Yet—Communications after the Crisis

The Importance of Follow-Through

One of the challenges cited by leadership in managing a crisis is what one might describe as "mission focus." In many cases leaders get so focused on the task required to complete the mission that the human aspects of the crisis can often get lost in the chaos. To a large extent, focusing on the mission and the tasks at hand should be the leader's focus, but it is communication that can enable leading successfully during a crisis situation, and effective communication has a huge level of significance for successfully resolving the situation as well as maintaining the morale of responders and everyone else affected by the crisis.[38]

The Right Stuff

Effective communication can be simply described as:

The right message, at the right time, delivered by the right person.

Crisis events tend to be inundated with information—facts are often wrapped in assumptions, opinions, and can often be completely wrong. This is especially true of any rapidly evolving situation. Take the time to verify and validate information. This fundamental leadership skill becomes critical in time of crisis and must be part of the planning process for critical incidents. Inconsistent communication from leadership is a common problem in a crisis. Messaging has to be clear and consistent—across all platforms and approaches.

Four key factors that increase trust and credibility for leaders in a crisis are:

- Caring and empathy
- Honesty and Openness
- Dedication or Commitment
- Expertise and Competence

All four of these factors can be demonstrated through communication.[39]

A Long Road

Once a crisis and the corresponding response has been completed, communication work is far from over. Depending on the nature of the emergency and response, communication needs might actually escalate. Being prepared and following good communication procedures will help.

In most cases, you may need to take time as a team to review what went well and what could have been done differently. Prioritize the list of improvements identified and follow up to make sure they are addressed. Consider sharing

> **Oxford High School, Oxford, Michigan**
>
> On November 30, 2021, at approximately 12:51 p.m., an identified student, 15, armed with a handgun, began shooting inside Oxford High School. Four people were killed (students); seven people (six students and one teacher) were wounded. The shooter was apprehended by law enforcement at the scene.
>
> www.fbi.gov

Figure 5.3. Oxford High School, Michigan. www.fbi.gov

a summary of this after-action review with parents, demonstrating the commitment to safety, transparency, and improvement.

If the emergency significantly impacted your school or district; someone was injured; or damage to the building occurred, provide updates consistently. Be sure to coordinate with your legal team.

If you experienced injuries (or worse), extensive damage to facilities, computer security compromise, or students out of school for multiple days, your postcrisis communications efforts will be demanding and extensive.

Parents, the community, the media, your school board, and local leaders will want answers to many questions: How did this happen, why did this happen, what could have been done differently, and what will be done so this does not happen again?

Formal investigations may occur, and media may remain outside the school to talk to parents, and it may be hard to focus on anything else.

If you are faced with this type of challenging situation, remain calm, factual, empathetic, and focused on learning and improvement. Be honest, transparent, and caring.[40]

Leadership in the Shadows

As the crisis at hand transitions from crisis management to consequence management, it remains critical that the leadership be visibly present, and a clear driving force behind the actions required to bring the community back to feeling whole again. The aftermath of a crisis is often a marathon and not a sprint. The crisis receives coverage in the media and garners public attention, but the restoration process that follows is challenging, because media and public (the unaffected public) interest often wanes. This is a critical time when leadership is necessary and is key to the success of the community rebounding from the crisis.

Conclusion

There are certainly a multitude of books covering crisis communications in detail. This chapter, and this book as a whole, is designed to expose school administrators to a spectrum of topics that will school thought leaders to take critical preplanning steps necessary to be able to respond appropriately during an event as well as manage the aftermath of a critical incident.

The technologies supporting and surrounding crisis communications continue to evolve, and the continued implementation of integrated technology platforms will certainly affect and enhance communications capabilities. Always be looking forward to bringing these new technologies and capabilities to bear at your school.

As with so many other things, the amount of time and effort spent in preparation for critical incidents will make these incidents much easier to manage. Routine familiarity with emergency protocols and procedures is paramount and close coordination and collaboration with partner agencies is absolutely critical.

The checklists at the end of the book will allow for a quick reference to some of the key topics and concepts discussed throughout the chapter.

Notes

1. Scott Gibson et al., "Communication, Communication, Communication: The Art of the Handoff," *Annals of Emergency Medicine*, December 7, 2009. https://doi.org/10.1016/j.annemergmed.2009.10.009.

2. Federal Commission on School Safety, "Final Report of the Federal Commission on School Safety," Presented to the President of the United States, December 18, 2018. https://www2.ed.gov/documents/school-safety/school-safety-report.pdf.

3. Ready.gov., "Crisis Communications Plans," 2023. https://www.ready.gov/business/emergency-plans/crisis-communications-plans.

4. Debra Davenport, "The 3 Most Effective Crisis Communication Strategies," *Purdue University Online Journal*, 2023. https://online.purdue.edu/blog/communication/effective-crisis-communication-strategies.

5. G. F. Böl, "Risk Communication in Times of Crisis: Pitfalls and Challenges in Ensuring Preparedness Instead of Hysterics," *National Library of Medicine*, 2015. https://pubmed.ncbi.nlm.nih.gov/26658329/.

6. John P. Jarvis and Brittany N. Murray, "Leadership During Crisis Response," *FBI Law Enforcement Bulletin*, May 8, 2019. https://leb.fbi.gov/articles/featured-articles/leadership-during-crisis-response-current-research.

7. U.S. Department of Homeland Security, "Understanding Risk Communication Best Practices. A Guide for Emergency Managers and Communicators," May 2012. https://www.start.umd.edu/publication/understanding-risk-communication-best-practices-guide-emergency-managers-and.
8. U.S. Department of Education, Office of Safe and Drug-Free Schools, "Practical Information on Crisis Planning," January 2007. http://www2.ed.gov/admins/lead/safety/emergencyplan/crisisplanning.pdf.
9. National Counterterrorism Center, "First Responder's Toolbox: Complex Operating Environment—Educational Facilities: Primary and Secondary Schools," June 28, 2019. https://www.dni.gov/files/NCTC/documents/jcat/firstresponderstoolbox/Complex_Operating_Environment_Education_Facilities_Primary_Secondary_Schools.pdf.
10. U.S. Department of Education, "Practical Information on Crisis Planning."
11. U.S. Department of Justice, Bureau of Justice Assistance, "Crisis Communications Quick Reference Guide," 2023. https://www.bja.gov/jag/.
12. U.S. Department of Education, "Practical Information on Crisis Planning."
13. U.S. Department of Justice, "Crisis Communications Quick Reference Guide."
14. Federal Commission on School Safety, "Final Report of the Federal Commission on School Safety."
15. California Office of Emergency Services, "California Emergency Management for Schools: A Guide for Districts and Sites," May 2023. https://resources.finalsite.net/images/v1696444581/sbceoorg/ld57piefrkwmmub8jwyi/California-Emergency-Management_A-Guide-for-Districts-and-Sites__Final-05-11-23-2.pdf.
16. Jarvis and Murray, "Leadership During Crisis Response."
17. Federal Commission on School Safety, "Final Report of the Federal Commission on School Safety."
18. Vincent A. Dalfonzo, "Focus on Crisis Management: Knowing the Adversary," *FBI Law Enforcement Bulletin*, October 2023. https://leb.fbi.gov/articles/focus/focus-on-crisis-management-knowing-the-adversary.
19. Chad C. Eldridge et al., "Communication During Crisis," *Nursing Management Journal*, 51, no. 8 (August 2020). https://journals.lww.com/nursingmanagement/FullText/2020/08000/Communication_during_crisis.9.aspx.
20. Jarvis and Murray, "Leadership During Crisis Response."
21. Hector-Neri Castaneda, *Actions, Imperatives, and Obligations* (Oxford University Press, 1967). http://www.jstor.org/stable/4544750.
22. Jarvis and Murray, "Leadership During Crisis Response."

23. Carrie A. Hall, "Mindfulness Breathing Strategies to Reduce Teacher Stress: A Mixed Method Study" (PhD diss., Missouri Baptist University, 2023). https://www.proquest.com/openview/3fc47abaed73dea4489f4a5be227255e/1?pq-origsite=gscholar&cbl=18750&diss=y.

24. Ron Duckworth, "How to Use the FBI's Behavioral Change Stairway Model to Influence Like a Pro," *EMS1 Journal*, May 2018. https://www.ems1.com/ems-training/articles/how-to-use-the-fbis-behavioral-change-stairway-model-to-influence-like-a-pro-c5W8CNGj5tuZZ0Av/.

25. Davenport, "The 3 Most Effective Crisis Communication Strategies."

26. Federal Emergency Management Agency, "Guide For Developing High-Quality School Emergency Operations Plans," 2013. https://rems.ed.gov/docs/School_Guide_508C.pdf.

27. National Counterterrorism Center, "First Responder's Toolbox."

28. Substance Abuse and Mental Health Services Administration, "Communicating in Crisis. Risk Communication Guidelines for Public Officials," Publication No. PEP19-01-01-005 (2019). https://store.samhsa.gov/product/communicating-crisis-risk-communication-guidelines-public-officials/pep19-01-01-005.

29. Ready.gov, "Crisis Communications Plans."

30. Federal Commission on School Safety, "Final Report of the Federal Commission on School Safety."

31. Substance Abuse and Mental Health Services Administration, "Communicating in Crisis. Risk Communication Guidelines for Public Officials."

32. Mustafa Emreet Civelek et al., "The Role of Social Media in Crisis Communication and Crisis Management," *International Journal of Research in Business & Social Science*, 5, no. 3 (2016). https://papers.ssrn.com/sol3/papers.cfm?abstract_id=3338292.

33. Mats Eriksson, "Lessons for Crisis Communication on Social Media—A Systematic Review of What Resea Tells the Practice," *International Journal of Strategic Communication*, 12, Issue 5 (August 30, 2018). https://doi.org/10.1080/1553118X.2018.1510405.

34. Substance Abuse and Mental Health Services Administration, "Communicating in Crisis. Risk Communication Guidelines for Public Officials."

35. Eriksson, "Lessons for Crisis Communication on Social Media—A Systematic Review of What Research Tells the Practice."

36. Substance Abuse and Mental Health Services Administration, "Communicating in Crisis. Risk Communication Guidelines for Public Officials."

37. Jarvis and Murray, "Leadership During Crisis Response."

38 Jarvis and Murray, "Leadership During Crisis Response."
39 Eldridge et al., "Communication During Crisis."
40 National School Public Relations Association, "The Complete Crisis Communication Management Manual for Schools," 2016. https://www.nspra.org/store/school-communication-benchmarking.

Bibliography

Böl, G. F. "Risk Communication in Times of Crisis: Pitfalls and Challenges in Ensuring Preparedness Instead of Hysterics." *National Library of Medicine*, 2015. https://pubmed.ncbi.nlm.nih.gov/26658329/.

California Office of Emergency Services. "California Emergency Management for Schools: A Guide for Districts and Sites," May 2023. https://resources.finalsite.net/images/v1696444581/sbceoorg/ld57piefrkwmmub8jwyi/California-Emergency-Management_A-Guide-for-Districts-and-Sites__Final-05-11-23-2.pdf.

Castaneda, Hector-Neri. *Actions, Imperatives, and Obligations*. Oxford University Press, 1967. http://www.jstor.org/stable/4544750.

Civelek, Mustafa Emreet et al. "The Role of Social Media in Crisis Communication and Crisis Management." *International Journal of Research in Business & Social Science*, 5, no. 3 (2016). https://papers.ssrn.com/sol3/papers.cfm?abstract_id=3338292.

Dalfonzo, Vincent A. "Focus on Crisis Management: Knowing the Adversary." *FBI Law Enforcement Bulletin*, October 2023. https://leb.fbi.gov/articles/focus/focus-on-crisis-management-knowing-the-adversary.

Davenport, Debra. "The 3 Most Effective Crisis Communication Strategies." *Purdue University Online Journal*, 2023. https://online.purdue.edu/blog/communication/effective-crisis-communication-strategies.

Duckworth, Ron. "How to Use the FBI's Behavioral Change Stairway Model to Influence Like a Pro." *EMS1 Journal*, May 2018. https://www.ems1.com/ems-training/articles/how-to-use-the-fbis-behavioral-change-stairway-model-to-influence-like-a-pro-c5W8CNGj5tuZZ0Av/.

Eldridge, Chad C., et al. "Communication During Crisis." *Nursing Management Journal*, 51, no. 8 (August 2020). https://journals.lww.com/nursingmanagement/FullText/2020/08000/Communication_during_crisis.9.aspx.

Eriksson, Mats. "Lessons for Crisis Communication on Social Media—A Systematic Review of What Research Tells the Practice." *International Journal of Strategic Communication*, 12, Issue 5 (August 30, 2018). https://doi.org/10.1080/1553118X.2018.1510405.

Farmer, Rob. "Critical Communication Issues During Disaster, MCI Response." *EMS1 Journal*, 2018. https://publications.ems1.com/2018/EMS1-eBook-Winter2018.pdf.

Federal Bureau of Investigation. "Crisis Communications—Quick Reference Guide," 2023. https://www.dhs.gov/sites/default/files/publications/fbi-crisis-communications-trifold-reference-guide.pdf.

Federal Commission on School Safety. "Final Report of the Federal Commission on School Safety." Presented to the President of the United States, December 18, 2018. https://www2.ed.gov/documents/school-safety/school-safety-report.pdf.

Federal Emergency Management Agency. "Guide For Developing High-Quality School Emergency Operations Plans," 2013. https://rems.ed.gov/docs/School_Guide_508C.pdf.

Gibson, Scott C., et al. "Communication, Communication, Communication: The Art of the Handoff." *Annals of Emergency Medicine*, December 7, 2009. https://doi.org/10.1016/j.annemergmed.2009.10.009.

Hall, Carrie A. "Mindfulness Breathing Strategies to Reduce Teacher Stress: A Mixed Method Study." PhD diss., Missouri Baptist University, 2023. https://www.proquest.com/openview/3fc47abaed73dea4489f4a5be227255e/1?pq-origsite=gscholar&cbl=18750&diss=y.

Jarvis, John P., and Brittany N. Murray. "Leadership During Crisis Response." *FBI Law Enforcement Bulletin*, May 8, 2019. https://leb.fbi.gov/articles/featured-articles/leadership-during-crisis-response-current-research.

National Counterterrorism Center. "First Responder's Toolbox: Complex Operating Environment—Educational Facilities: Primary and Secondary Schools," June 28, 2019. https://www.dni.gov/files/NCTC/documents/jcat/firstresponderstoolbox/Complex_Operating_Environment_Education_Facilities_Primary_Secondary_Schools.pdf.

National School Public Relations Association. "The Complete Crisis Communication Management Manual for Schools," 2016. https://www.nspra.org/store/school-communication-benchmarking.

Pennybacker, Gail M. C. J. "Focus on Social Media: Communication as a Function of Leadership." *FBI Law Enforcement Bulletin*, March 2019. https://leb.fbi.gov/articles/focus/focus-on-social-media-communication-as-a-function-of-leadership.

Ready.gov. "Crisis Communications Plans," 2023. https://www.ready.gov/business/emergency-plans/crisis-communications-plans.

Substance Abuse and Mental Health Services Administration. "Communicating in Crisis. Risk Communication Guidelines for Public Officials." Publication No. PEP19-01-01-005, 2019. https://store.samhsa.gov/product/communicating-crisis-risk-communication-guidelines-public-officials/pep19-01-01-005.

U.S. Department of Education, Office of Safe and Drug-Free Schools. "Practical Information on Crisis Planning," January 2007. http://www2.ed.gov/admins/lead/safety/emergencyplan/crisisplanning.pdf.

U.S. Department of Homeland Security. "Understanding Risk Communication Best Practices. A Guide for Emergency Managers and Communicators," May 2012. https://www.start.umd.edu/publication/understanding-risk-communication-best-practices-guide-emergency-managers-and.

U.S. Department of Justice, Bureau of Justice Assistance. "Crisis Communications Quick Reference Guide," 2023. https://www.bja.gov/jag/.

6 Principal Leadership during School Shootings
Ensuring Safety and Support

The role of a principal extends far beyond the administrative tasks of operations and daily activities in a school building. The Wallace Foundation summarizes two of the five key responsibilities of a principal as (1) shaping the vision for academic success for all students, and (2) creating a climate hospitable to education.[1] Core to academic success and a climate hospitable to education is shaping a safe and secure environment conducive to learning. From prevention to response, school safety and providing a safe and secure environment demand utmost attention in the broader landscape of educational leadership.

In the unfortunate event of a school shooting, the role of the principal becomes even more important. Effective principal leadership during such an incident is crucial in ensuring safety, limiting injuries, and reducing the possibility of loss of life. Principals are at the helm of leading their staff, students, parents, and community through an incident as well as the long, difficult recovery process. This starts and ends with established trust, transparency, and communication.

This chapter explores the importance of principal leadership in prioritizing and maintaining school safety and the effective strategies they employ in the event of an incident.

> Quick Tip: Principals are at the helm of leading their staff, students, parents, and community through an incident as well as the long, difficult recovery process. This starts and ends with established trust, transparency, and communication.

Setting Expectations and Developing Policies

As the school's primary "safety officer," each building principal is responsible for creating a sense of security by implementing policies and procedures ensuring that students, teachers, and parents feel safe.[2]

This is more than a goal in a plan that's sitting on a shelf, acquiring dust as the daily workload piles up. Parents want to know how their child's school is prepared in the event of trauma or danger, and strong administrators understand this. It is the principal's responsibility to ensure that teachers and staff have taken all necessary precautions and have a plan that has been routinely drilled by both students and teachers.[3]

When students view organizational crisis threats as anticipated and crisis management as well-planned, they will be more resilient and less susceptible to traumatic stress.[4] Plans must be made to reestablish support systems, reconnect students with parents and other caregivers, and encourage a return to normal routines.

Oftentimes, principals feel that decisions about safety protocols are out of their control, driven instead by state legislatures, superintendents, local law enforcement, and school boards.[5]

> Quick Tip: The principal is the literal closest person to the parents, students, teachers, and broader school community questioning the safety of the school and how prepared the school is for a safety incident.

A threat of violence to a school, whether internal or external, can escalate to the unimaginable category quickly. And while planning and practicing for this scenario is mandatory in nearly all states in today's school environment, a principal should serve as a trusted and guiding force in setting clear expectations and developing comprehensive safety policies.[6]

By establishing an atmosphere of trust and accountability, the principal creates a foundation for open communication among students, teachers, and parents. In addition, this extends to all school community members understanding the safety protocols, such as emergency procedures, lockdown drills, and adherence to safety standards. Transparency and consistent reinforcement of these policies instill a sense of security within the school community.

Promoting Trust Within the School Community

The principal influences the overall climate of a school, playing a crucial role in ensuring a positive and inclusive learning environment.[7]

A safe school environment is fostered through inclusive practices, mutual respect, and promoting a culture of diversity, equity, and acceptance. Foundations of trust are essential in every aspect of principal leadership. But nowhere is more essential than preparing for scenarios of violence than a school setting. Every student, staff member, parent, and community member must trust that the principal is preparing every day for the unimaginable. There are many ways to build trust every day over time.

> Quick Tip: Transparency and consistent reinforcement of these policies instill a sense of security within the school community.

Trust starts in small everyday interactions from the principal in the school. "Building leadership trust begins with personal trustworthiness."[8] Leaders need to consistently do these three things:

1. Do what they say they will do.
2. Acknowledge mistakes quickly and openly.
3. Confront conflicts between personal values and the professional environment.[9]

The principal then allows openness to vulnerability to be seen. There must be a genuine and authentic demeanor from the principal. Principals must be seen as trustworthy, and genuinely listen and reflect on others' ideas, whether a student, staff member, or community member. This vulnerability is the foundation for establishing a climate of trust necessary for the students, staff, and community to respond during a school crisis.

Simple Ways to Begin to Build Trust

Principals should know their staff members and students by name and know something important about each of them. The message is clear: "The principal thinks I am an important member of the community and has made an effort to know something that is important to me." By greeting staff and students by name in the morning, welcoming them for the day, and wishing them a good evening as they are leaving at the close of the day, the principal becomes a real person. The door for communication is open.

Principal leaders invest in initiatives that encourage the building of positive relationships, resolving conflicts peacefully, and implementing proactive anti-bullying measures across the school. This creates not only an environment of trust but also one with a sense of family and community for every member of the school. Another aspect of safety is students feeling safe from bullying, harassment, and intimidation. A safe school climate is imperative for students to take ownership in keeping each other safe. Ensuring that staff treat students and each other with respect and care is a major part of a safe school climate. Safe school climates provide a better opportunity for students to "see something, say something" preventing more serious situations from unfolding.[10]

> Quick Tip: A safe school climate is imperative for students to take ownership in keeping each other safe. Ensuring that staff treat students and each other with respect and care is a major part of a safe school climate.

Exhibiting Trust Through Characteristics

Personality matters. If students in a school can describe their principal as having certain characteristics, the students are more likely to respond to the principal's expectations and guidance in a crisis situation at the school.[11]

There are companion surveys for parents and staff that would measure the level of trust for the principal. These characteristics include the following as posed in a Student Trust Survey:

The principal in the school . . .

1. Likes students
2. Is fair
3. Is there for students
4. Makes me feel safe
5. Tells the truth to students
6. Does the right thing
7. Can be trusted

Imagine the following. (1) Staff and students believe that the principal is this trustworthy person. (2) There is transparency about the safety drills and practices with students and staff. And (3) Feedback is considered, and when appropriate, adjustments are made. Now imagine the unimaginable. Imagine there was an incident in the school and safety contingencies were activated. If the characteristics are there, and the protocols are in place, every possible option to protect students and mitigate harm or death could be engaged with high levels of trust in the leader, reducing the chaos and increasing chances of students surviving.

> Quick Tip: By encouraging open lines of communication, the principal fosters an environment in which students feel safe reporting suspicious behavior or concerns.

This all begins with the leader knowing staff and students, engaging with them daily, and being vulnerable to the school community. Unfamiliarity with team members (i.e., staff), and a lack of relationships with staff have been cited as presenting challenges even experienced leaders could face. "Lack of familiarity with the team was identified as a leadership challenge because delegating becomes difficult due to a lack of knowledge of team members' skill sets or how best to interact with these personnel."[12]

> Quick Tip: Practice, practice, practice of safety drills accompanied by the principal talking through the "why" of each drill, each time, increases the engagement of the students. Students are at the center of it all and play a role in safety! Don't leave them out!

Communication, Collaboration, and Partnerships

Collaboration and partnerships cannot be built without trust. However, trust, communication, and collaboration among the principal, teaching staff, parents, and students are critical to maintaining school safety. During a school shooting, clear and effective communication is crucial for the safety and well-being of all individuals involved.

Principals must quickly activate their emergency response protocols, ensuring that staff members (and, reasonably, students) know the situation and can implement their assigned roles. This includes coordinating with law enforcement agencies, sharing important information with teachers, monitoring the situation in real time, and disseminating accurate updates to parents and the wider community. Open lines of communication aid in minimizing confusion and panic, allowing the principal to maintain control and foster a sense of security. A common denominator in school safety incidents is that students and administrators use their cell phones to text, email, or post information on social media. Generally, nearly every 911 call from a school originates from a cell phone. This communication platform can be used by schools to address emergency situations as well as less serious situations, such as hallway disturbances, plumbing malfunctions, and updates on classroom or club activities.[13]

Universities employ this communication system and with careful training, parent support, and district support, using cell phones as a primary communication tool could be successfully employed. And when thousands of Texans spent the night on the roofs of their homes to escape floodwaters during Hurricane Harvey, "Twitter provided something visible; the exquisite word choices gave them something to hold onto. The portability of the platform was vital."[14]

> Quick Tip: A strong leader will work collaboratively with staff and local law enforcement to develop and regularly update comprehensive emergency response plans.

By encouraging open lines of communication, the principal fosters an environment in which students feel safe reporting suspicious behavior or concerns. Principals who actively engage teachers in professional development opportunities related to safety equip them with the knowledge and skills to address potential threats effectively. By collaborating with parents and community organizations, principals can address safety concerns, utilizing external resources to enhance overall school safety, as well as increase trust in the principal.[15]

Practice, practice, practice of safety drills accompanied by the principal talking through the "why" of each drill, each time, increases the engagement of the students. Students are at the center of it all and play a role in safety! Don't leave them out!

Parent communication needs to include regular updates on safety planning and practice. This communication will build support for parents to remind their children to take the planning and practices seriously. By discussing the importance of safety and the effort and energy devoted to keep students and staff safe, parents see the principal as a trusted and authoritative figure in safety and trust that they will be informed quickly and often in the event of a breach of safety in the school. While safety protocol and practice details must be limited, the open lines of communication are not.

Experts recommend incorporating redundancy into the system; having a critical message disseminated over multiple systems will make it less likely that someone who needs to be alerted will not get the news. Among the possible communications paths: automated telephone messages; email notices; text messages to cell phones; district websites; websites of local public safety agencies; two-way radio systems, broadcast radio and television stations; electronic billboards; sirens or alarms.[16]

These communication paths must be incorporated into regular communication with parents in order to familiarize parents with the communication tools.

If everyone knows their part in maintaining safety in the school, the school will perform as a prepared team in times of chaos and violence; much the same as first responders simulate crisis situations to practice best practices. Creating this environment with students, staff, parents, and community will ensure the best chance of survival.

Creating a Culture of Preparedness

A proactive school community starts with a principal who understands the importance of emergency preparedness. A strong leader will work collaboratively with staff and local law enforcement to develop and regularly update comprehensive emergency response plans. These plans should include protocols specific to active shooter situations, ensuring a coordinated and effective approach in the event of an incident. Principal leadership in conducting drills, training staff, and educating students about emergency procedures will further empower the school community to respond swiftly and confidently.

Although it may be a shared responsibility in many schools, in the end, it is the principal's responsibility to ensure, develop, and maintain up-to-date safety plans that encompass all potential threats, from natural disasters to intruders or violence.[17]

There are specifics required of these plans depending on your city, state, or municipality. These plans will be comprehensive and should be continuously reviewed and practiced ensuring their effectiveness. Principals work closely with the school community and safety experts to design emergency response plans, conduct regular drills, and train staff members in safety protocols. By staying informed about the latest safety technologies, principals can implement systems such as video surveillance, controlled access, and anonymous tip reporting, further enhancing school safety.

The broadest category of school safety is physical safety, which refers to the physical features of a building or environment, such as access, control, and security.[18]

Physical safety is an important element of school safety as it shapes the environment where students spend most of their time. Strategies to improve

> **Saugus High School, Santa Clarita, California**
>
> On November 14, 2019, at approximately 7:38 a.m., an identified student, 16, armed with a handgun, began shooting classmates at Saugus High School. Two people (students) were killed; three people (students) were wounded. The shooter shot himself at the scene before law enforcement arrived; he died at a hospital the following day.
>
> www.fbi.gov

Figure 6.1. Saugus High School, California. www.fbi.gov

physical safety may also serve as the first line of defense for school safety incidents of all severities.

> Quick Tip: By being visible, approachable, and accessible, principals build stronger relationships with students, staff, and parents. This fosters a sense of trust and ensures that students feel supported and safe.

This component of creating readiness is not one that is a task on a checklist. These training and practice drills need to accompany the principal being transparent with students each time a drill is practiced and include them as the center of the practices. This is a continuation of the trust that is built every day by the leader that strengthens the effectiveness of the safety plans and drills.

Safety means many things to many people in a school setting. Every definition carries importance. Physical safety can be supported with the tactical items, by (1) making sure external facility and safety inspections are complete and repairs are completed, (2) having correctly working fire extinguishers or alarms, and (3) making sure the building locks and security safeguards are in working order.

Maintenance of the building is also critical to ensure heating and cooling equipment, electrical, natural gas equipment, and plumbing are properly working and supporting the needs of the students and staff. A well-maintained building will support well-planned and practiced safety protocols being employed with the highest level of effectiveness.

> Quick Tip: The immense responsibility entrusted to principals calls for continuous professional development and ongoing reassessment of practices to adapt to evolving safety risks.

Trust Through Presence and Interaction

Earlier, you read the example of greeting students and staff in the morning and saying goodbye at the end of the day to build a strong school community. An effective principal is present and actively engaged within the school community. By being visible, approachable, and accessible, principals build stronger relationships with students, staff, and parents. This fosters a sense of trust and ensures that students feel supported and safe. Principals also work closely with local law enforcement agencies, fostering partnerships that contribute to a safer campus environment. By having a strong presence both online and in-person, principals can promptly address safety concerns and communicate relevant updates to the school community.

Supporting Staff and Students

A principal's role extends beyond responding to a critical incident. Emotional support for staff, students, and families is an integral aspect of effective leadership before, during, and after a school shooting. Principals must prioritize the well-being of everyone affected, including themselves! Principals must be prepared to communicate with staff members, guiding them through the process of healing. By ensuring that resources are made available to support regaining staff mental and emotional health, principals lead staff to being available for students. For students, principals should work collaboratively with counselors and mental health professionals to establish safe spaces where they can openly express their thoughts and feelings, reassuring them that their concerns and fears are valid and being addressed. The principal should expect and ensure that central office personnel will be fully available to help provide these necessary resources for recovery.

Rebuilding Trust and Resilience

During the long road to recovery from a school shooting, principals should work closely with teachers, parents, and community leaders to create long-term action plans that focus on security enhancements, mental health support, and ongoing training to ensure the overall safety and well-being of everyone involved. This comes full circle as the culture of preparedness and trust will need to be rebuilt with all school stakeholders! Creating a high trust environment and keeping safety plans and practice drills at the forefront with staff, students, and parents is paramount to reducing the chances of an active shooter incident. When that trust is breached, starting again to build the community of trust and safety is the focus of recovery.

> Quick Tip: The premise of this work (safety implementation plan) is not compliance. The premise is that leadership and trust are necessary to create a school culture and environment that will increase the likelihood of each student in the school returning home to their families each night.

No one knows better the challenges and opportunities of rebuilding trust following a school safety incident at their school. Wesley Weaver, the principal at Licking Valley High School in Newark, Ohio, and Andy Jacks, principal at Ashland Elementary School in Manassas, Virginia, took opportunities with their school communities to hear firsthand how they were processing the event following the well-known mass school shooting in Parkland, Florida.[19] Showing this authentic interest and sensitivity to parents' concerns set the stage for continued trust in their principals, paving the way for two-way communications, engagement, and an effective threat response in their own schools.

Bringing It All Together

Principal leadership plays a pivotal role in safeguarding the welfare and security of students. By setting clear expectations, developing comprehensive safety policies, promoting a trusting school climate, fostering collaboration and partnership, creating and updating safety plans, and maintaining a visible and active presence, principals establish a culture of safety within schools. The immense responsibility entrusted to principals calls for continuous professional development and ongoing reassessment of practices to adapt to evolving safety risks. When principals effectively lead with a focus on school safety, students can thrive in an environment that encourages growth, development, and well-being. Dufresne and Dorn sum up the everyday work in a school that provides a culture of openness, trust, communication, and resilience that combat violence in schools.

> *Jerilyn Dufresne*: How can school personnel connect with youth who are vulnerable to gang influence, school failure, and delinquency?
>
> *Michael Dorn*: First, on an environmental basis, you can design, structure, and operate schools in a manner that makes them warm and caring places where children can succeed. Academic success is critical when we talk about intervention strategies such as keeping kids out of gangs. We can do this through building design, through policies, through how we structure and design a school, and the way we operate it. Second, on a personal level, we can constantly advocate for children and serve as cheerleaders for all who work with children. More people may become too narrowly focused on one thing they are doing. We are not just teaching these kids math or

English, but we are helping them succeed and overcome adversity. The third thing we can do, again on a personal level, is reach out to individual children. A child who has a close connection with a caring responsible adult can often overcome incredible odds. Children are very resilient when they have this type of support. As we advocate for children, we can make a difference. When a student who has been bullied tells us, "I made it because of you. I stayed in school because of you," there may be 50 to 100 others who stayed in school because of that staff member but never said anything.[20]

It is unbelievable sometimes how much of a difference a bus driver, a teacher, a teacher's aide, or someone who works in the cafeteria can make

Edmund Burke School, Washington, D.C.

On April 22, 2022, at approximately 3:28 p.m., an identified shooter, 23, armed with a handgun and two rifles, began shooting at people at the Edmund Burke School. Four people were wounded (including one security officer). The shooter committed suicide at the scene after the arrival of law enforcement.

www.fbi.gov

Figure 6.2. Edmund Burke School, Washington, DC. www.fbi.gov

if they have the right attitude and reach out, reclaiming children and youth. It is astounding, but often, they see the problems but do not realize the remarkable good they do.[21]

Preparing students and staff for those times will build trust and faith that every eventuality has been thoroughly considered and prepared for, the staff and students' voices heard, and that each member of the school community is important. As a school leader, the goal is to ensure students go home to their parents every day. The same is expected of our own children's principals.

Theory Into Practice: Safety Implementation Plan

Principals need to be efficient and effective with their time. Interpretation and application of what this chapter discusses takes time. The following is a step-by-step guide, with examples of what a school safety plan could look like. The premise of this work is not compliance. The premise is that leadership and trust are necessary to create a school culture and environment that will increase the likelihood of each student in the school returning home to their families each night. This type of preparation becomes ingrained in the day-to-day expectations and operations for staff and students and is embraced as a way to keep the students and staff in the best possible position to survive any type of school safety emergency.

Preparation and training are explicitly planned and professional development for all staff is intertwined throughout the year in various modalities: face-to-face training, emails, practice drills, discussions, and debriefings to improve the safety plans. Does this commitment mean less time on other school goals and priorities? Making safety the top priority of staff and students does not mean missing out on academic achievement or developing a culture of support and caring. In fact, making safety a priority enhances both achievement and a caring, inclusive culture. Why, you might be asking. According to Dr. Willam Glasser, a considerable influence in leadership development, humans have five basic needs: survival (physical) belonging, respect, freedom, and joy (social needs). In the application to the school setting, this translates to students and staff feeling safe and that they are part of the school family, they have a genuine voice, are respected, and find joy and satisfaction in their achievements.[22]

Glasser's Choice Theory explains the "why" of prioritizing safety and the steps that follow will explain the "how."

During twenty-seven years of serving as a building administrator, there were fire, tornado warnings, and outside threats where leadership, trust, and well-practiced drills paid off. Real events may happen at inconvenient times (the start and end of the school day, recess, lunch, or between classes). These different scenarios of time and place need to be explicitly addressed to staff and students.

Step 1. List all the drills required by your state and district for the academic year. An example might look like this:

Inside threats are a whole different event. For example, if a school gets a note or phone bomb threat or a warning of a shooting, there is no sure way to identify if it is coming from a member of the student/school community. Schools have different protocols in place to reduce the possibility of weapons or other destructive devices coming inside the school. Despite their best thinking and efforts, a shooter will find a way around the efforts to keep the students safe. Once the shooter breaches the perimeter of the school, the opportunity to protect students and staff is minimized, and injuries or loss of life is probable.

Hence, the best defense against active shooter situations is on the preventive end. Every member of the school community must genuinely feel valued and respected. The effort it takes from the principal to move toward that goal is monumental. The effort to establish the culture that every human is important is critical to reduce the chances of an inside active shooter emerging from the school community. The work toward this goal starts with principal self-efficacy and the commitment to develop every school staff member with skills to authentically embrace every student, every minute of every day. Students need at least a connection to one trusting adult in the building. If the school community can achieve that, it is one important key to preventing an inside active shooter situation. As you review in your mind, the school shootings that have happened since Columbine in 1999, you will be hard-pressed to find one where the shooter is engaged in academics, cocurricular activities and has a group of students that share a lunch table or after school time together.

Table 6.1. Required Drills

Types of safety drills*	Required number per year**	Full practices	Walkthrough/talkthrough practices
Fire	9	9	1 (prior to first drill) over PA or during beginning of year class meetings
Tornado	4 (usually seasonal)	4	3 (1st of year class meetings, 2nd during early fall, and 3rd second semester prior to March)
Earthquake	2	2***	1st (prior to the first drill) over PA or during the beginning of year class meetings. Suggested two additional talkthroughs by providing staff with a script and have each teacher in a pre-selected class time, show the class sign and identifying vest or apparel, review class leader responsibilities and ask students if they have any questions.
Lockdown (outside threat)	2	2****	Use varied methods to review monthly. Class meetings, principal-prepared PA walkthroughs, and prepared classroom walkthroughs should be calendared and reviewed in staff meetings.
Lockdown (inside threat)	2	2****	Use varied methods to review monthly. The most vital component of preparing students and staff for an inside threat rests with the principal. Calendar and prepare staff and students for when these talkthroughs will happen. The trust factor is critical. Specific details will be discussed later in the chapter.

Participation in Homeland Security County Wide Drills and/or Participation in Local First Responders District or School Wide Drills	The opportunity may be provided to your school. Having students and staff participate in both experiences. The result is the school community becoming closer and learning to appreciate first responders and trust one another.	Usually a onetime event. Preparation with the principal, staff, and students can take some effort. Communicating with parents and allowing a student to opt out is critical for building trust. The debrief after the drill is crucial for students, staff, and parents to explain what was learned and how safety protocols have been improved.	Building a relationship with county and local first responders is a safe but effective way to help staff, students and parents understand that safety is a top priority. Developing maps including schools' entrances with first responders can be downloaded to the first responders' vehicles and cut response time in the case of an actual event. The learning that occurs for the first responders is akin to the learning that occurs when emergency rooms go through drills to prepare for multiple casualty events. The pride that the staff and students feel for contributing to increasing community safety builds trust with first responders and school leadership.

** Required drills will vary by state and district. Use a formula that every month you will prepare students and staff by using full drills and primarily walkthrough or talkthrough drills. Building trust with staff and students requires walkthroughs and talkthroughs to be in the front of their minds in a calm and disciplined manner. It is important to practice drills during lunch, recess, between classes, and before and after school. Use the talkthroughs on the PA or in the school cafeteria to make sure staff and students know the variations of the safety protocols during non-classroom times.

*** Required earthquake drills may be district wide and requires a significant amount of time to complete. Therefore, practice walkthrough may not be practical. However, talkthroughs in a class meeting setting should include a map of the evacuation plan to an open space (generally, on athletic fields) and the actual signs and apparel of the class leader so students know where to line up outside and where to report of they are separated from their group.

**** Required lockdown drills can be triggering for some students. Prepare staff for what the classroom will look like prior to the full practices. The principal plays a key role in these drills. The message needs to be clear and nonthreatening. The drills are in place in case of an unexpected and improbable inside or outside threat. Give examples of what an outside threat looks like (examples include: a robbery at a nearby bank or business, a suspect on foot or in a car near the school, an area wide police matter that is in the vicinity of the school). These types of events precipitate precautions to mitigate any possibility of impact to the students and staff in a school. Depending on the specifics of the situation, students may stay put in their classrooms and continue with instruction or may be asked to move away from windows and doors. The principal is key to transparency and calm. Students hear in the principal's voice they are going to be fine, and that the precautions of an outside threat will continue to be monitored and updates on the PA will be provided. Principals need to consider the age of their students and what will be most effective in the situation.

****Inside threats are a different circumstance, and preparation needs to be managed quite differently. Inside threats will be discussed in more detail in other chapters. The most important leadership and trust lesson to take away from this chapter is that actions you take every day can reduce the chance of a current or former student engaging in a violent attack at the school. If, as a leader, students believed that the school cared for their needs of survival, belonging, respect, freedom, and joy the need for them to seek satisfying those needs in an extreme, violent way in the school setting will be reduced. Guaranteed? No, never guaranteed but reduced.[23]

> Quick Tip: The skill of leading staff to take every opportunity to support a healthy school environment is at the heart of building trust with staff.

Mental health issues are complex as well as individualized to the person, and simple solutions are generally not effective. The effort and energy it takes to build a trusting, caring community in a school is not by employing programmed social-emotional curriculum but by investing in every staff member to develop skills to effectively build healthy and strong relationships with each other and with students. Certainly, a packaged program may give an opportunity to open the conservations about what it might take to connect with every student and colleague. The packaged programs can include early warning detection for a troubled student. But school-wide implementation is usually not consistent and can seem disingenuous to some students. So, what does it take for every school staff member to believe that they can make a difference to their students?

Effective Internal Communication During Safety Drills and Actual Events

In a crisis situation, the principal, office staff, custodial staff, and assistant administrators will most likely not be in the office area or in close proximity to each other. The PA system in a school usually has one or at most, two, access points and broadcasts. In cases of external threats, tornado warnings, and fires, the PA system might be most efficient, if accessible. Practice run-throughs with staff and students will help in these situations. An exception would be a PA system that broadcasts on speakers outside the building. If there is an external threat, then the PA system should not be used. In the case of an internal threat, there are a few reasons to use the PA system. The back up to the PA system could be email but only if every staff member could access school email on their cell phones. The most practical method of communication for any safety situation is text messages in selected groups or an ALL-staff text message. If the staff is trained and knows how text messaging will be used, it could move groups of students in selected room groupings quickly and quietly. This protocol should be practiced as well. Text messaging should be used when the PA system or email is not available or practical. Examples of these situations are outlined below:

- In the case of a fire, students and staff exit the building to pre-assigned areas. Any instructions needed after the exit is completed will be done by texting. When the fire department arrives and determines which school entrance will be used, students may need to be relocated to accommodate the first responders or under fire department orders, students and staff may need to move farther away from the building. Natural gas leaks, or other causes of explosions and fire would result in needing to move students farther away.
- Earthquake drills usually have students exit to a field or athletic field away from the school. No other practical means of communication exist except text messaging. In the case of an actual earthquake, cell towers may likely be disabled.
- Tornado drills have students in hallways or restrooms away from windows. If in the case of a tornado warning and damage to the building, electricity will most likely be lost, again, leaving text messaging as the best option for communication.
- External threats are generally managed by total lockdown with outside and inside doors locked. Using the PA system only broadcasting inside the building is practical. The principal voice remaining calm and being transparent can be the best option.
- Internal threats with an aggressor can best be managed through text messaging groups. The principal can message different areas of the building by presetting groups with different instructions, if that is the best way to mitigate the damage and reduce the number of students and staff hurt or injured. Each district will have recommended policies to use in internal threat scenarios. In the actual event, teachers will do what they can to protect the students in their care. The more staff are trained, and options discussed, the more confident they will be in planning to put their students in the safest position.

Building Trust with Staff

Every member of school staff has the opportunity to support or hamper a healthy school environment every minute they are in the building. The skill of leading staff to take every opportunity to support a healthy school environment is at the heart of building trust with staff. The Glasser Choice Theory and meeting the five basic needs and Megan Tschannen-Moran's Facets of Trust have much in common with each other on how to build reciprocal relationships of trust in a building.[24]

The table describes behaviors in a school that will build trust. The leader is responsible for setting the example, following through with coaching staff on how to interact in the culture and not resort to deviating from the components. To say this is easy is an understatement. The work of building trust with staff is an everyday effort on the leader's part. There can be no back steps in this work. The building of trust, however, is the cornerstone of a strong safety plan. There is no working around it. Every action that a leader takes must match the components. If there is a misstep, the leader must own it immediately, take responsibility, and offer no excuses. Some examples of what this looks like in action:

- Don't be a boss, be a leader. Trust is not built by telling adults what to do but by including them in what is expected in the school environment. I equate this to the age old discussion of what to do with student tardiness. The principal wants the teachers to manage it, the teachers want the principal to manage it, and the only people who can improve their tardiness is the student. Time and energy for endless discussions blaming adults has never offered a solution. There are temporary solutions to reduce tardiness, but they are not usually sustainable. The discussion needs to be centered around what the staff can do to make getting to classes more important than being late. Include students in the discussion through focus groups. This is leadership.

> Quick Tip: Don't be a boss, be a leader. Trust is not built by telling adults what to do but by including them in what is expected in the school environment.

- When there are teacher–parent disputes over a teacher–student interaction, the conference can be really tense. The principal siding with the teacher or the parent is a recipe for an unsatisfactory conclusion. Prepare to ask questions that focus the dispute on what each party expects from the conference. Identify what the needs of each party are and guide an honest discussion to allow each party to come together and a plan to move forward. Sometimes, it reveals incorrect information, sometimes it involves a genuine apology for a misunderstanding, and mostly it is about having the teacher and parent realize the humanity of one another and agree on how to move forward.

- The same example can be used with a teacher-teacher dispute or a teacher–staff member dispute.
- Lastly, offer solutions and support to staff issues like arriving late, leaving early, missing staff meetings, unwillingness to collaborate with peers, refusing to follow curriculum, and behavioral or social expectations in the school setting. Blaming or accusing the staff member will invoke the defense mechanism for survival. Positive outcomes for adult behavior

Table 6.2. The Glasser Choice Theory and Megan Tschannen-Moran's Facets of Trust

Tschannen-Moran Facets of Trust	Glasser Five Basic Needs*	Practical definition of what trust and leadership look like in a school
Benevolence	Belonging	Reciprocal caring for one another, expecting and receiving positive intentions, fairness, confidentiality, and acceptance.
Honesty	Belonging	Honoring promises, agreements, and straight forward conversations without manipulation from either participant.
Openness	Power	Honoring and respecting the voices in the room without judgment. Genuinely listening to all perspectives with consideration.
Reliability	Freedom	Dependable to do what you say you will do with fidelity. Predicable behavior once an agreement is determined.
Competence	Joy	Having the skills and knowledge to think critically, solve problems and deliver on leadership by example.

*Aligns with the four social needs of Glasser Choice Theory, not the physical need of survival.

changes come from them and their realization of their impact of not changing. The principal role in this setting is coach.

Building Trust with Students

Building trust with students is based on the same Facets of Trust and Choice Theory's five Basic Needs as building trust with staff and parents.[25]

However, daily actions by the principal and staff must be able to be seen with students. Here are some examples of building trust with students:

- Be transparent with students about the components of trust and why it is important to you (principal and staff). An effective practice includes spending time at the beginning of each year teaching students explicitly what to expect from the principal and staff and what students are expected to contribute to the culture. Then refer to this messaging every day and throughout the school day in classes, lunch and recess, assemblies, and one-on-one interactions. The more students hear the messaging, and it is matched by adult behavior, and students are held to the standards set the more productive the school year will develop over time.

> Quick Tip: A most important example of building trust is for the principal to host a series of student focus groups that vary the membership each time. Using random selection processes to do this will ensure that the different students in diverse groups will have a chance to have their voices heard. There is no substitute for students knowing they belong to their school family when creating a safe and caring environment.

- Celebrate students in a genuine and authentic way. Many do not do the usual celebrations like student of the month, athlete of the week, honor roll, and so on. Celebrations were focused on individualized student achievement and growth. For example, pep rallies or class or grade-level assemblies honored students for their in school and out of school achievements. Becoming an Eagle Scout or dancing in the city ballet company production of "The Nutcracker" are accomplishments. Not more or less important than school accomplishments and these need to be celebrated. Heroes are all ages. They need to be recognized in their school community. Volunteering weekly at the animal shelter or working at camps for younger children or participating in 4-H and county fair competitions need to be celebrated. Knowing each student and honoring their contributions inside and outside of school build trust that each student is important. Birthday celebrations are important too. Everyone has one but to each person that day is special. Celebrate often and genuinely. Students can tell if you mean it!

- Notice the needs of students and take action to meet those needs. The cafeteria manager may open her doors early for students whose parents had to get to work earlier than school started. The students helped get the morning routine set up and had social time under the care of a staff member. This early entry became extremely important and appreciated by the students and their parents. They now belonged and had their school family.
- Students whose families did not have washers and dryers at home came to school with dirty clothes on, alienating them from their peers. The solution was to buy a washer and dryer at school and provide students with a chance to do their laundry. It was low key, and staff helped out with changing loads, folding the clothes, and getting it back to the student privately. This one small action sent the message that we cared about our students
- Students who were going home to little or no food were supported by staff and the lunch program providing weekend meal bags sent home in backpacks on Fridays. Low-key, again, but the need was met, and students trusted the school was there for them.
- To have assemblies or grade-level events, providing each student with a school spirit shirt to wear on those days provided every student to be part of the action! Certainly, have loaners for students who forgot or didn't have access to wearing the shirt that day.

Quick Tip: Keeping parents informed of how the drills and practices will be included as part of the school day is critical. Details are not necessary or recommended. What is necessary and recommended is that parents know that state or district required drills will be augmented with walk-throughs and talkthroughs throughout the year.

- Providing supplies and school opportunities that do not rely on parents providing them. Nothing screams inequity more than creating a culture of "haves" and "have nots." Preplanning and accessing school business and parent organization relationships to provide a welcoming and equitable experience where there is no shame or embarrassment for students.

- A most important example of building trust is for the principal to host a series of student focus groups that vary the membership each time. Using random selection processes to do this will ensure that the different students in diverse groups will have a chance to have their voices heard. The topics can vary from group to group but should always be centered on checking to see if student basic needs are being addressed. The principal should always provide food and drinks during these thirty-minute sessions. The sessions should be done in nonclass times (advisory, lunch, recess, homeroom, etc.). The subliminal message is that academics are a priority. A survey of students' ideas for the focus group topics can help provide a meaningful and relevant experience for the students. This does take time and preparation but to students their voices are listened to, respected, and valued. There is no substitute for students knowing they belong to their school family when creating a safe and caring environment.

Building Trust with Parents

Keeping parents informed of how the drills and practices will be included as part of the school day is critical. Details are not necessary or recommended. What is necessary and recommended is that parents know that state or district required drills will be augmented with walkthroughs and talkthroughs throughout the year. The purpose of the totality of the drills and augmented practices should be clearly articulated to parents; the more students and staff practice, the less there will be panic or chaos in the unlikely event of a real need for the use of a safety protocol and/or evacuation. There are ways that districts provide principals to keep parents informed. Learn to use the resources that parents prefer. Several ways to send the same information will increase the number of parents who receive and respond. Offering remote sessions for parent group meetings, parent-teacher conferences, and for information sharing will appeal to parents who need babysitting for younger children in order to get to the school. Survey parents several times a year and ask them what will help them help their students. Use different methods of gathering data. Trust is built when the school interacts with parents in a genuine and caring way that meets the parents' needs of accessibility.

Notes

1. Wallace Foundation, "Five Key Responsibilities—The School Principal as Leader: Guiding Schools to Better Teaching and Learning," February 2012. https://www.wallacefoundation.org/knowledge-center/pages/key-responsibilities-the-school-principal-as-leader.aspx.
2. Texas A&M International University Online, "School Administrators Teaching Safety," *The International University of Journal*, November 12, 2019. https://online.tamiu.edu/programs/education/ms-edu-admin/administrators-need-to-know-about-safety/.
3. Texas A&M International University Online, "School Administrators Teaching Safety."
4. S. E. Broc, Q. Ballard, and C. Saad, *Preparing for and Responding to Disasters* (New York: Routledge, 2013).
5. National Center on Safe Supportive Learning Environments, "School/District Administrators," accessed June 2, 2024. https://safesupportivelearning.ed.gov/training-technical-assistance/roles/schooldistrict-administrators.
6. J. Wilkins, "50-State Comparison: K-12 School Safety," *Education Commission of the States*, 2022. https://www.ecs.org/50-state-comparison-k-12-school-safety-2022/.
7. National Center for Learning Disabilities, "Inclusive Principal Leadership—Part 1: What It Is & Why It Matters," May 17, 2022. https://ncld.org/?s=Inclusive+Principal+Leadership+%E2%80%93+Part+1%3A+What+it+is+%26+Why+it+Matters+.
8. D. B. Reeves, *From Leading to Succeeding: The Seven Elements of Effective Leadership in Education* (Solution Tree Press, 2016).
9. Reeves, *From Leading to Succeeding: The Seven Elements of Effective Leadership in Education*.
10. National Center on Safe Supportive Learning Environments, "School/District Administrators."
11. M. Tschannen-Moran, *Trust Matters, Leadership for Successful Schools*, 2nd ed. (Jossey-Bass, 2004).

12. John P. Jarvis and Brittany N. Murray, "Leadership During Crisis Response," *FBI Law Enforcement Bulletin*, May 8, 2019. https://leb.fbi.gov/articles/featured-articles/leadership-during-crisis-response-current-research.

13. D. Davis, "Rapid Communications are the Key to School Safety," *District Administration*, July 24, 2022. https://districtadministration.com/rapid-communications-are-the-key-to-school-safety/.

14. Gail M. C. J. Pennybacker, "Focus on Social Media: Communication as a Function of Leadership," *FBI Law Enforcement Bulletin*, March 2019. https://leb.fbi.gov/articles/focus/focus-on-social-media-communication-as-a-function-of-leadership.

15. J. Sebastian et al., "Principal Leadership and School Performance: An Examination of Instructional Leadership and Organizational Management," *Leadership and Policy in Schools*, October 29, 2018. https://doi.org/10.1080/15700763.2018.1513151.

16. American School and University, "Security Solutions: The Colors of Crisis," accessed June 2, 2024. https://www.asumag.com/safety-security/crisis-disaster-planning-management/article/20851025/security-solutions-the-colors-of-crisis.

17. Wallace Foundation, "Five Key Responsibilities—The School Principal as Leader: Guiding Schools to Better Teaching and Learning."

18. National Institute of Justice, "Synthesizing Knowledge on Equity and Equity-based School Safety Strategies," accessed June 2, 2024. https://nij.ojp.gov/library/publications/synthesizing-knowledge-equity-and-equity-based-school-safety-strategies.

19. E. Blad, "What Principals Can Do to Keep Schools Safe Amid Shooting Fears," *Education Week*, October 17, 2018. https://www.edweek.org/leadership/what-principals-can-do-to-keep-schools-safe-amid-shooting-fears/2018/10.

20. Jerilyn Dufresne and Michael Dorn, "Crisis Prevention. Keeping Students and Schools Safe," *Reclaiming Children and Youth: The Journal of Strength-based Interventions*, 14, no. 2 (Summer 2005): 93.

21. Dufresne and Dorn, "Crisis Prevention. Keeping Students and Schools Safe."

22. C. Salus, "Applying Glasser's Choice Theory to Classroom Management," *Study.com*, April 18, 2017. https://study.com/academy/lesson/applying-glassers-choice-theory-to-classroom-management.html.

23. Salus, "Applying Glasser's Choice Theory to Classroom Management."

24. Tschannen-Moran, *Trust Matters, Leadership for Successful Schools*.

25. Salus, "Applying Glasser's Choice Theory to Classroom Management."

Bibliography

American School and University. "Security Solutions: The Colors of Crisis." Accessed June 2, 2024. https://www.asumag.com/safety-security/crisis-disaster-planning-management/article/20851025/security-solutions-the-colors-of-crisis.

Blad, E. "What Principals Can Do to Keep Schools Safe Amid Shooting Fears." *Education Week*, October 17, 2018. https://www.edweek.org/leadership/what-principals-can-do-to-keep-schools-safe-amid-shooting-fears/2018/10.

Brock, S. E., Q. Ballard, and C. Saad. *Preparing For and Responding to Disasters*. New York: Routledge, 2013.

Davis, D. "Rapid Communications are the Key to School Safety." *District Administration*, July 24, 2022. https://districtadministration.com/rapid-communications-are-the-key-to-school-safety/.

Dufresne, Jerilyn, and Michael Dorn. "Crisis Prevention. Keeping Students and Schools Safe." *Reclaiming Children and Youth: The Journal of Strength-based Interventions*, 14, no. 2 (Summer 2005): 93.

Jarvis, John P., and Brittany N. Murray. "Leadership During Crisis Response." *FBI Law Enforcement Bulletin*, May 8, 2019. https://leb.fbi.gov/articles/featured-articles/leadership-during-crisis-response-current-research.

National Center for Learning Disabilities. "Inclusive Principal Leadership—Part 1: What It Is & Why It Matters," May 17, 2022. https://ncld.org/?s=Inclusive+Principal+Leadership+%E2%80%93+Part+1%3A+What+it+is+%26+Why+it+Matters+.

National Center on Safe Supportive Learning Environments. "School/District Administrators." Accessed June 2, 2024. https://safesupportivelearning.ed.gov/training-technical-assistance/roles/schooldistrict-administrators.

National Institute of Justice. "Synthesizing Knowledge on Equity and Equity-based School Safety Strategies." Accessed June 2, 2024. https://nij.ojp.gov/library/publications/synthesizing-knowledge-equity-and-equity-based-school-safety-strategies.

Pennybacker, Gail M. C. J. "Focus on Social Media: Communication as a Function of Leadership." *FBI Law Enforcement Bulletin*, March 2019. https://leb.fbi.gov/articles/focus/focus-on-social-media-communication-as-a-function-of-leadership.

Reeves, D. B. *From Leading to Succeeding: The Seven Elements of Effective Leadership in Education*. Solution Tree Press, 2016.

Salus, C. "Applying Glasser's Choice Theory to Classroom Management." *Study.com*, April 18, 2017. https://study.com/academy/lesson/applying-glassers-choice-theory-to-classroom-management.html.

Sebastian, J., E. Allensworth, W. Wiedermann, C. Hochbein, and M. E. Cunningham. "Principal Leadership and School Performance: An Examination of Instructional Leadership and Organizational Management." *Leadership and Policy in Schools*, October 29, 2018. https://doi.org/10.1080/15700763.2018.1513151.

Texas A&M International University. "School Administrators Teaching Safety." *The International University of Journal*, November 12, 2019. https://online.tamiu.edu/programs/education/ms-edu-admin/administrators-need-to-know-about-safety/.

Tschannen-Moran, M. *Trust Matters, Leadership for Successful Schools.* 2nd ed. Jossey-Bass, 2004.

Wallace Foundation. "Five Key Responsibilities—The School Principal as Leader: Guiding Schools to Better Teaching and Learning," February 2012. https://www.wallacefoundation.org/knowledge-center/pages/key-responsibilities-the-school-principal-as-leader.aspx.

Wilkins, J. "50-State Comparison: K-12 School Safety." *Education Commission of the States*, 2022. https://www.ecs.org/50-state-comparison-k-12-school-safety-2022/.

7 Concluding Thoughts and Recommendations

This book considered school safety, which is important and timely because incidents of targeted violence in schools in the United States are becoming common rather than rare occurrences, and solid leadership is needed to effectively manage them if and when they occur.

School safety has always been important. It comprises a broad variety of situations for which schools are responsible, such as planning for natural disasters, implementing anti-bullying programs, recognizing potential suicides and responding in the unfortunate case they occur, working with law enforcement, and overseeing medical emergency responses. This book illuminated the relationships among the component school safety challenges. Here are some concluding thoughts and recommendations.

First and of utmost importance is to know and understand the "chain of command" (and perhaps the term "unity of command") which means that all respondents operate under a single commander who has the requisite authority to direct all respondents employed in pursuit of a common purpose.[1] In a military context, the chain of command is the line of authority and responsibility along which orders are passed within a military unit and between different units. The chain of command is the sequence of leaders through which command is exercised and executed. The term is also used in a civilian management context describing comparable hierarchical structures of authority. Such structures are included in fire departments, police departments, and other organizations that have a paramilitary command or power structure.[2]

Response to all crises requires a clear chain of command among all responders. The Incident Command System (ICS) is based on the premise that every crisis has certain major elements requiring clear lines of command and control.[3] ICS is a widely applicable management system designed to enable effective, efficient incident management by integrating a combination of facilities, equipment, personnel, procedures, and communications operating within a common organizational structure.[4]

ICS is a standardized approach to the command, control, and coordination of emergency response, providing a common hierarchy within which responders from multiple agencies can be effective. ICS was initially developed to address problems of interagency responses to wildfires in California. It is now a component of the National Incident Management System (NIMS) in the United States, where it has evolved into use in all-hazards situations, ranging from active shootings to hazmat scenes. NIMS is a standardized approach to incident management developed by the U.S. Department of Homeland Security (National Incident Management System, 2024).[5]

In addition to the chain of command, also of great importance is the team constructed to plan and respond to crises. Each school crisis response team must reflect the skills, abilities, education, and professional experiences necessary to respond effectively if and when crises arise. School and school district leaders/administrators must identify the roles and the persons who would be involved in planning and responding to school crises. Along with others, those persons would include city and county emergency planners, campus police, social workers, counselors, psychologists/mental health professionals, student behavior managers, and teachers from related education levels. Parent and student liaisons would be included on the planning teams. Others who would be involved in planning and responding to crises would be the building/facility managers, transportation managers, secretaries, a chaplain/clergy member, a school public affairs professional, and the school nurse.

Other key factors in crisis response are internal and external communication and information management—both the means of communicating and the content. Because schools exist within the context of a larger community, it is important that response teams establish and maintain open lines of communication with community partners. A coordinated approach is especially critical when an incident receives broad traditional and social media coverage and when the community is looking to the schools for guidance, support, answers, and leadership.[6]

Communication is a crucial part of successful crisis management. Withholding or delaying the release of information significantly and unnecessarily increases anxiety for many important groups of people. It also greatly reduces the reputation of the school district and its employees. A single poorly managed crisis can easily ruin decades of goodwill built by the school district.[7]

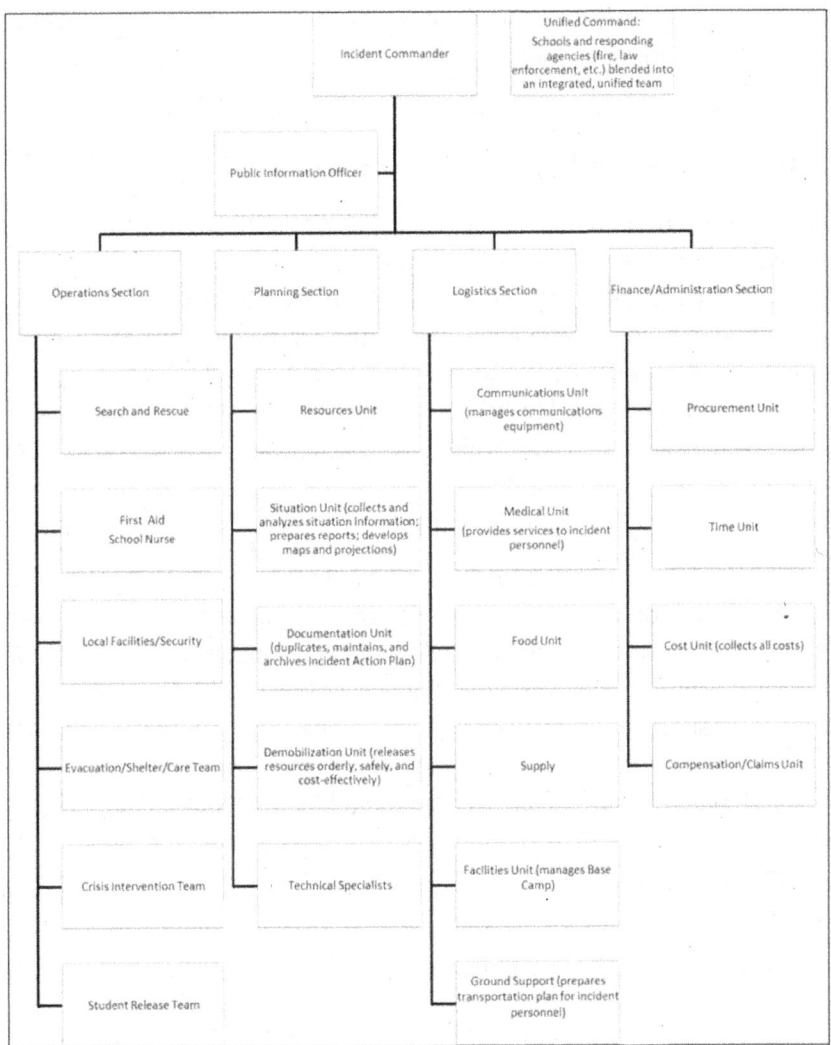

Figure 7.1. Example Incident Command Structure for a School Incident. Dr. David E. Johnson www.trainbeready.com

It is important to remember the underlying principle for successful crisis communication: "Tell it all, and tell it fast." In the event of a crisis, schools and districts must immediately establish themselves as the best source of information. Failing to provide information during a crisis quickly creates rumors. Unless the school district provides information quickly, a crisis will generate many unsubstantiated rumors that many people will assume are true. In order to prevent rumors, it is important to remember two well-known truths about crisis communication:

- "In the absence of information, misinformation becomes news."
- "If you don't speak for yourself, someone else will."[8]

Emergency communications procedures/protocol in the event of an incident would include maintaining a list of local law enforcement agencies and designating and authorizing someone to contact the agencies. Emergency procedures would also include a system and the medium for informing all principals and school personnel within a school district. Such emergency procedures would describe how to contact/inform parents, guardians, or persons in parental relation to the students. Emergency communications procedures would also include how to report, employ, and respond to mass media.[9]

Critically, crisis planners and responders must integrate disparate law enforcement and emergency response communication technologies/devices to ensure compatibility/interoperability to enable effective communication between agencies during crises. In the event of electronic communications failures, crisis planners and responders should also consider hard-copy means of communication delivered by runners. Whether electronic or physical, crisis planners and responders should consider creating and using prepared templates tailored to specific recipients to quickly compose and communicate critical information.

Planners and responders should collaborate with key students to identify and monitor relevant social networking sites. Social media can be used to disseminate important and accurate information. Schools can strategically use social media to share prevention-oriented safe messaging, and to offer support to students who may be struggling to cope, and to identify and respond to students.[10]

Also in these concluding thoughts and recommendations is the strong recommendation that school crisis response teams develop and use checklists. A checklist is a type of job aid used in repetitive tasks to reduce failure by compensating for potential limits of human memory and attention. Checklists are used both to ensure safety-critical system preparations are carried out completely and in the correct order, and to ensure no step is left out of a procedure. Checklists help ensure consistency and completeness in carrying out a task. A basic example of a checklist is the "to do list."[11]

School crisis planning and response teams should develop checklists for every anticipated incident specific to the role of each team member. For example, the school public affairs professional's checklist might include:

- Collect accurate information.
- Compose notification letter.
- Notify persons in parental relation to a student.
- Report to mass media.
- Designate an assembly area to accommodate a news conference.
- Monitor social media.

Campus police's checklist might include:

- Implement crowd control procedures.
- Implement traffic control procedures.
- Establish a security perimeter.

School safety is important. School principals and officials are not alone. There is a proliferation of federal, state, and local agencies ready to assist school officials.

A final concluding thought and recommendation is to create multiple "Gotta Go," "Crisis," "Grab and Go," or "Bug-Out" kits or bags with supplies one might need in an emergency (New York State Education Department, 2013).[12] The contents would include a copy of the emergency procedures, first-aid supplies, rosters, communication devices, telephone numbers, clipboards, and prepared templates. The bags would be placed in different locations within the school and one at each evacuation site for ready, emergency accessibility.[13]

In closing, this book introduced the background of the challenge of school safety to include trends, unresolved issues, and broad associated concerns. It included analyses of school violence, the effects of school violence on students, common characteristics of public mass shooters, the shortcomings of law enforcement, the idiosyncrasies of electronic communications and technology, schools' responsibility for student safety, the controversial and negative policy intervention termed zero-tolerance, the heightened attention given to the physical environment and hardening, whether responses and drills are effective or simply harmful, soft and hard controls and school climate, and, finally, the challenge of implementing evidence-based violence-prevention programs.

Notes

1. "Unity of Command," in Wikipedia, December 2, 2024. https://en.wikipedia.org/wiki/Unity_of_command.
2. "Command Hierarchy," in Wikipedia, December 2, 2024. https://en.wikipedia.org/wiki/Command_hierarchy.
3. New York State Education Department, *New York State School Safety Guide*, 2013.
4. Homeland Security, *National Incident Management System* (U.S. Department of Home Security, 2008).
5. "National Incident Management System," in Wikipedia, December 2, 2024. https://en.wikipedia.org/wiki/National_Incident_Management_System.
6. American Foundation for Suicide Prevention/Suicide Prevention Resource Center Workgroup, *After a Suicide Tool Kit for Schools* (Author, 2011).
7. S. Rausch, *Project SAVE Ithaca City School District District-Wide Safety Plan 2013–2014*, 2013.
8. Rausch, *Project SAVE Ithaca City School District District-Wide Safety Plan 2013–2014*.
9. The University of the State of New York, *Guide for School Safety Plans*, 2001.
10. American Foundation for Suicide Prevention/Suicide Prevention Resource Center Workgroup.
11. "Checklist," in Wikipedia, December 2, 2024. https://en.wikipedia.org/wiki/Checklist.
12. New York State Education Department.
13. Office of Safe and Drug-Free Schools, *Practical Information on Crisis Planning: A Guide for Schools and Communities*. U.S. Department of Education, 2007.

Bibliography

American Foundation for Suicide Prevention/Suicide Prevention Resource Center Workgroup. *After a Suicide Tool Kit for Schools*. Author, 2011.

"Checklist." Wikipedia, December 2, 2024. https://en.wikipedia.org/wiki/Checklist.

"Command Hierarchy." In Wikipedia, December 2, 2024. https://en.wikipedia.org/wiki/Command_hierarchy.

Homeland Security. *National Incident Management System*. U.S. Department of Home Security, 2008.

"National Incident Management System." In Wikipedia, December 2, 2024. https://en.wikipedia.org/wiki/National_Incident_Management_System.

New York State Education Department. *New York State School Safety Guide*, 2013.

Office of Safe and Drug-Free Schools. *Practical Information on Crisis Planning: A Guide for Schools and Communities*. U.S. Department of Education, 2007.

Rausch, S. *Project SAVE Ithaca City School District District-Wide Safety Plan 2013–2014*, 2013.

The University of the State of New York. *Guide for School Safety Plans*, 2001.

Appendices

Appendices

Appendix A
FBI School Active Shooter Incidents 2019–2023

University of Nevada, Las Vegas (UNLV), Las Vegas, NV
On December 6, 2023, at approximately 11:45 a.m., an identified male shooter, sixty-seven, armed with a handgun, began shooting people at UNLV in Las Vegas, Nevada. Three people (employees) were killed; one person (a visiting professor) was wounded. The shooter was killed by law enforcement at the scene following an exchange of gunfire.

Covenant Presbyterian School, Nashville, TN
On March 27, 2023, at approximately 10:13 a.m., an identified female/transgender male shooter, twenty-eight, armed with two rifles and a handgun, began shooting people inside and outside Covenant Presbyterian School in Nashville, Tennessee. Six people (three students and three faculty) were killed; one person (a law enforcement officer sustained incidental injuries) was wounded. The shooter was killed by law enforcement at the scene.

Michigan State University, East Lansing, MI
On February 13, 2023, between 8:18 p.m. and 8:30 p.m., an identified male shooter, forty-three, armed with a handgun, began shooting people at Michigan State University in East Lansing, Michigan. Three people (students) were killed; five people (students) were wounded. The shooter died by suicide at another location after law enforcement arrived.

Central Visual and Performing Arts High School, St. Louis, MO
On October 24, 2022, at approximately 9:11 a.m., an identified shooter, nineteen, armed with a rifle, began shooting at people at the Central Visual and Performing Arts High School. Two people were killed (one teacher and one student); seven people (students) were wounded. The shooter was killed by law enforcement after an exchange of gunfire at the scene.

Robb Elementary School, Uvalde, TX
On May 24, 2022, at approximately 11:32 a.m., an identified shooter, eighteen, armed with a rifle, began shooting at people at Robb Elementary School. Twenty-one people were killed (nineteen students, two teachers); seventeen people were wounded (including three law enforcement officers). The shooter was killed by law enforcement after an exchange of gunfire at the scene.

Gwinnett County School Bus, Suwanee, GA
On May 9, 2022, at approximately 7:15 a.m., an identified shooter, fifty-seven, armed with a gun, began shooting at people on a bus in a residential neighborhood. One person was wounded (bus driver, an employee). The shooter was apprehended by law enforcement at another location.

Edmund Burke School, Washington, DC
On April 22, 2022, at approximately 3:28 p.m., an identified shooter, twenty-three, armed with a handgun and two rifles, began shooting at people at the Edmund Burke School. Four people were wounded (including one security officer). The shooter committed suicide at the scene after the arrival of law enforcement.

Rigby Middle School, Rigby, ID
On May 6, 2021, at approximately 9:08 a.m., an identified student, twelve, armed with a handgun, began shooting inside and outside Rigby Middle School. Three people (including two students and a school employee) were wounded. The shooter was apprehended by law enforcement at the scene after being disarmed and restrained by a teacher.

Oxford High School, Oxford, MI
On November 30, 2021, at approximately 12:51 p.m., an identified student, fifteen, armed with a handgun, began shooting inside Oxford High School. Four people were killed (students); seven people (six students and one teacher) were wounded. The shooter was apprehended by law enforcement at the scene.

STEM School Highlands Ranch, Highlands Ranch, CO
On May 7, 2019, at approximately 1:50 p.m., an identified student, eighteen, armed with a rifle and a handgun, and a second identified student, sixteen,

armed with two handguns, allegedly began shooting in two different locations at the STEM School Highlands Ranch. After one student was killed during a confrontation with the first shooter, two other students subdued and disarmed the shooter, thereby ending the threat posed by that shooter. The second shooter wounded six students before being detained and disarmed by a private security officer. One person (a student who confronted one of the shooters) was killed; eight people (students) were wounded (including two students who were accidentally shot by a private security officer). Both shooters were apprehended by law enforcement in different locations at the school.

Saugus High School, Santa Clarita, CA
On November 14, 2019, at approximately 7:38 a.m., an identified student, sixteen, armed with a handgun, began shooting classmates at Saugus High School. Two people (students) were killed; three people (students) were wounded. The shooter shot himself at the scene before law enforcement arrived; he died at a hospital the following day.

Data provided by FBI Active Shooter Reports from 2019 to 2023.
https://www.fbi.gov/how-we-can-help-you/active-shooter-safety-resources
#FBI-Resources

Appendix B
Online References (January 2025)

FBI.Gov

    Active Shooter Resources

    https://www.fbi.gov/how-we-can-help-you/active-shooter-safety-resources

    Violence Prevention in Schools, March 2017

    https://www.fbi.gov/file-repository/violence-prevention-in-schools-march-2017.pdf/view

    Making Prevention a Reality: Identifying, Assessing, and Managing the Threat of Targeted Attacks

    https://www.fbi.gov/file-repository/making-prevention-a-reality.pdf/view

USSS.Gov

    National Threat Assessment Center

    https://www.secretservice.gov/protection/ntac

    Improving School Safety Through Bystander Reporting

    https://www.secretservice.gov/newsroom/reports/threat-assessments/schoolcampus-attacks/details-1

    Behavioral Threat Assessment Units: A Guide for State and Local Law Enforcement to Prevent Targeted Violence

    https://www.secretservice.gov/sites/default/files/reports/2024-10/Behavioral-Threat-Assessment-Units-A-Guide-for-State-and-Local-Law-Enforcement-to-Prevent-Targeted-Violence.pdf

    Averting Targeted School Violence: A U.S. Secret Service Analysis of Plots Against Schools

    https://www.secretservice.gov/newsroom/reports/threat-assessments/schoolcampus-attacks/details-0

CISA.Gov

https://www.cisa.gov/topics/physical-security/active-shooter-preparedness

READY.Gov

https://www.ready.gov/campus

Readiness and Emergency Management for Schools (REMS) Technical Assistance (TA) Center

https://rems.ed.gov/

Prior Knowledge of Potential School-Based Violence: Information Students Learn May Prevent a Targeted Attack

https://rems.ed.gov/docs/doe_bystanderstudy.pdf

Timeless School Safety Strategies

https://rems.ed.gov/docs/Timeless-Strategies-Fact-Sheet_508C.pdf

Guide For Developing High-Quality School Emergency Operations Plans

Federal Emergency Management Agency, 2013

https://rems.ed.gov/docs/School_Guide_508C.pdf

National Association of School Psychologists

www.nasponline.org

National Education Association (NEA) School Health and Safety

https://www.nea.org/healthy-schools

National Association of School Resource Officers (NASRO)

https://www.nasro.org/

SchoolSafety.gov

https://www.schoolsafety.gov/

Partner Alliance for Safer Schools

https://passk12.org/

Ten Essential Actions to Improve School Safety

https://portal.cops.usdoj.gov/resourcecenter/content.ashx/cops-w0891-pub.pdf

National Parent Teacher Association (PTA)

https://www.pta.org/home/family-resources/safety/School-Safety

Practical Information on Crisis Planning: A Guide for Schools and Communities

http://www2.ed.gov/admins/lead/safety/emergencyplan/crisisplanning.pdf

FEMA Exercise and Preparedness Tools

https://www.fema.gov/emergency-managers/national-preparedness/exercises/tools

Final Report Of The Federal Commission On School Safety

Presented to the PRESIDENT OF THE UNITED STATES

https://www2.ed.gov/documents/school-safety/school-safety-report.pdf

Leadership During Crisis Response

FBI Law Enforcement BulletIn

https://leb.fbi.gov/articles/featured-articles/leadership-during-crisis-response-current-research

Complex Operating Environment—Educational Facilities: Primary and Secondary Schools

National Counterterrorism Center First Responder's Toolbox

https://www.dni.gov/files/NCTC/documents/jcat/firstresponderstoolbox/Complex_Operating_Environment_Education_Facilities_Primary_Secondary_Schools.pdf

Appendix C
Training Exercise Checklist

- The Number One Training Requirement is SAFETY. Every Exercise Needs a Safety Plan.
- Discussion-based exercises: These are used to familiarize participants with current plans, policies, and procedures, or may be used in the development of new plans.
  - Tabletop Exercises involve key personnel discussing realistic, but hypothetical, scenarios in an informal and stress-free environment. This form of exercise can be used to assess current plans, procedures, or systems and help to identify strengths and areas in need of improvement.
- Operations-based exercises: These are characterized by an actual reaction to a simulated scenario, a response to emergency conditions, mobilization of apparatus, resources, and commitment of personnel.
  - Drills are coordinated, supervised exercise activities normally used to test a single specific operation or function. Schools commonly conduct fire evacuation drills, but a comprehensive approach to emergency management also requires practicing other procedures (shelter-in-place, lockdown, etc.) under various conditions.
  - Functional Exercises are like drills but involve multiple partners. These types of exercises are conducted in a realistic environment without the movement of personnel and equipment.
  - Full-Scale Exercises are the most complex type of exercise. They are multiagency, multi-jurisdictional, multi-organizational exercises that validate many facets of preparedness. Full-scale exercises are conducted in real time, creating a stressful, time-constrained environment that closely mirrors real events.

Appendix D
Sample Emergency Contact List

School

- Office
- Principal
- Assistant Principal(s)
- School Nurse
- Counselor
- Cafeteria
- Psychologist
- School-Based Law Enforcement Resource Officer
- Facility Manager
- Maintenance/Janitorial

District

- District Emergency Management Coordinator
- District Safety
- District Public Information Officer
- Superintendent, Asst. Superintendent
- School Resource/ Liaison Officer
- Facilities
- Food Services
- Transportation Director

- Human Resources
- Finance

Public Safety

General Emergency = 911

- Law Enforcement
  - Emergency: 911 (and local number is available)
  - Dispatch:
- Fire
  - Emergency: 911 (and local number is available)
  - Dispatch:
- Emergency Medical Services
- Poison Control
- Hospital

Public Utility Emergency Numbers

- Power (Electric)
- Natural Gas
- Water
- Municipal Government Utility District

Appendix E
Sample Administrator's "Go Bag" Checklist

Personal

- Personal Cell Phone
- Personal Emergency Contact List
- Extra Medications
- Change of Clothes and Hat
- Travel Toiletry Kit
- Flashlight w/ Extra Batteries
- Charger & Cables for ALL electronics and cell phone
- Multipack of water bottles
- Energy bars or other protein snacks
- Instant coffee packs
- Climate-Appropriate Items (hand warmers, sunscreen, rain gear or other clothing, etc.)
- Individual First-Aid Kit and/or Stop the Bleed Kit
- School
- School or District-issued cell phone
- School or District-issued radio
- School Emergency Plan
- Diagram of the entire campus and surrounding area
- School Map (with the following information on the map):
- Diagram of the entire campus site and surrounding areas.
    - Primary evacuation routes
    - Alternate evacuation routes

- Handicap evacuation areas
- Utility access/shut-offs for:
  - Gas
  - Water
  - Electricity
  - HVAC System
  - Telephone System
- Site Assignments and Staging Areas
- Hazardous Material storage areas
- Heat plants/boilers
- Room numbers
- Door/window locations
- Know the location of blueprints for the site. These may be necessary in tactical situations.
- Local Area Map (city or county)
- Paper, Pens, Dry-Erase Markers
- Clipboard
- Laptop
- Emergency Contact List(s).
- Emergency information for students and staff.
- Account and login information for website, social media, and communication platforms.
- District-issued vest and/or ID badge
- Master Keys [or have immediate access to who has them]

Appendix F
Sample Crisis Communications Checklist

Before the Crisis

Maintain updated contact lists for all area Public Information Officers (PIOs).

- Police, Fire, Emergency Medical, Hospitals.
- City officials, schools, public venues, district, and so on.
- Names, titles, and all phone and email information.

Pre-identify methods available for joint communications.

- Email lists, conference call capabilities at each agency.
- Develop MOUs with surrounding agencies to assist with media response.
- Obtain proper names and titles for all agency chiefs.

Obtain local media contact information, including means to deliver press releases.

At the Beginning of the Crisis

Request additional media assistance from the District.

- Staff to answer phones, manage press conferences, maintain a media log, coordinate with Incident/Unified Command, navigate social media, and write press releases and talking points.

Determine what information can be released in the first minutes in coordination with first responder agencies.

Establish coordination among PIOs.

- Identify and contact PIOs from all entities affected.
- Agree to a preferred method for joint communications and whether email chain, bridge line, conference calls.
- Agree to limit investigative information release to agencies on a need-to-know basis.
- Identify single agency and phone numbers to which all media calls will be referred for official information. (This can change later but pick one to start.)
- Identify an agreed-upon recontact time.
- Agree on information, if any, that may be released while initial coordination efforts are underway.

Appendix G
Sample Press Conference Checklist

- Be prepared. Proactively manage your emotions. Be honest. Be brief. Be accessible.
- Understand all the facts, especially technical ones, and stick to them.
- Keep cool. Do not become defensive; do not lose your temper or argue.
- Develop a written statement to be read and handed out.
- Pause and collect your thoughts before you respond to reporters' questions.
- Words have consequences. Use the right words.
- Don't babble. Know what to say. Say it, and then repeat it.
- If you don't know the answer, stop talking.
- Use common and clear language. Avoid using educational terminology or acronyms.
- Expect everything you say to appear in print or electronic media.
- Never lie.
- Don't make promises you can't keep.
- Stress concern for student safety and positive actions taken by the school or district.
- Know what is being done to help staff and students manage the situation.
- Do not make statements about responsibility until all the facts are known.
- Avoid using no comment. Explain why you can't answer.

- Saying "I don't know" is an acceptable response and can actually build credibility.
  - Immediately follow the "I don't know" with a statement that explains why you don't know (e.g., early in the investigation) and when and how you will provide further information to answer the questions.
- Don't speculate, guess intent, or accept assumptions.

Working with the Media

- The interview is not over until the reporter leaves. Always be careful about what you say in the presence of a reporter before or after an interview. The microphone may still be on.
- Do not speak "off the record." The cost can be too high if that agreement is not respected.

Glossary

Access And Functional Needs (AFN): Individual circumstances requiring assistance, accommodation or modification for mobility, communication, transportation, safety, health maintenance, due to any temporary or permanent situation that limits the ability of an individual (such as a person with disabilities) to take action in an emergency.

After-Action Report: A document that captures the incident or exercise scenario and actions of the whole school/campus community and community partners. The purpose is to synthesize information and data from the emergency event or exercise, recognize strengths, determine areas of improvement, and generate potential corrective actions.

Agency: A government element with a specific function offering a particular kind of assistance.

Area Command: An organization that oversees the management of multiple incidents or oversees the management of a very large or evolving situation with multiple ICS organizations. See *Unified Area Command*.

Assignment: A task given to a person or team to perform based on operational objectives defined in the Incident Action Plan (IAP).

Assisting Agency: An agency or organization providing personnel, services or other resources to the agency with direct responsibility for incident management.

Association of Threat Assessment Professionals (ATAP): The Association of Threat Assessment Professionals (ATAP) is as a nonprofit organization of law enforcement, mental health professionals, and other security experts involved in the area of threat and violence risk assessment.

Behavioral Threat Assessment: A fact-based investigative and analytical approach that focuses on what a particular individual is doing and saying, and not on whether the individual "looks like" those who have attacked schools in the past. Threat assessment emphasizes the importance of such behavior and communications for identifying, evaluating, and reducing the risk posed by an individual who may be thinking about or planning for a school-based attack.

Branch: The organizational level having functional or geographical responsibility for major aspects of incident operations. A branch falls between the Section Chief and the division or group in the Operations Section, and between the section and units in the Logistics Section. FEMA uses Roman numerals or functional areas to identify branches.

Chain of Command: The orderly line of authority within the ranks of incident management organizations.

Clear Text: Communication that does not use codes. See *plain language*.

Command: The act of directing, ordering, or controlling by virtue of explicit statutory, regulatory, or delegated authority.

Command Staff: A group of incident personnel that the Incident Command or Unified Command assigns to support the command function at an Incident Command Post (ICP). Command Staff often include a PIO, a Safety Officer, a Liaison Officer and any assistants they may have.

Contagion: Violent incidents often lead to more violent incidents in a short period of time.

Continuity of Operations (COOP): As defined in the National Continuity Policy Implementation Plan (NCPIP) and the National Security Presidential Directive-51/Homeland Security Presidential Directive-20 (NSPD-51/HSPD-20), COOP is an effort within individual executive departments and agencies to ensure that Primary Mission Essential Functions (PMEF) continue to occur during a wide range of emergencies, including localized acts of nature, accidents and technological or attack-related emergencies.

Copycat Effect: Copycats are individuals who attempt to copy previous violent acts, such as school shootings. There is typically an increase in copycat threats and actions immediately following a highly publicized violent incident.

Credentialing: Providing documentation that identifies personnel and authenticates and verifies their qualification for a particular position.

Crime Prevention Through Environmental Design (CPTED): An approach to directly modify the environment to take advantage of preexisting environmental assets or change the design features and condition of particular targets (e.g., school buildings, doors, and windows) or areas in an effort to reduce crime. Natural Surveillance, Natural Access Control, Territoriality Reinforcement, and Management and Maintenance are key principles of CPTED.

Critical Infrastructure: Assets, systems, and networks, whether physical or virtual, so vital to the United States that their incapacitation or destruction would have a debilitating impact on security, national economic security, national public health or safety, or any combination of those matters.

Director: The ICS title for an individual responsible for supervising a branch. Also, an organizational title for an individual responsible for managing and directing the team in an EOC.

Disaster Recovery Reform Act (DRRA): Part of the Federal Aviation Administration Reauthorization Act of 2018. The DRRA aims to improve FEMA's disaster preparedness, response, recovery and mitigation programs and build the nation's capacity for future catastrophic events.

Emergency: Any incident, whether natural, technological, or human caused, that necessitates responsive action to protect life or property.

Emergency Management Assistance Compact (EMAC): A congressionally ratified agreement that provides form and structure to interstate mutual aid. Through EMAC, a disaster-affected state can request and receive assistance from other member states quickly and efficiently, resolving two key issues up front: liability and reimbursement.

Emergency Management Institute (EMI): FEMA's national focal point for the development and delivery of emergency management training to enhance the capabilities of officials from SLTT governments and volunteer organizations.

Emergency Operations Center (EOC): The physical location where the coordination of information and resources to support incident management (on-scene operations) normally takes place. An EOC may be a housed in a temporary facility or in a permanently established, central facility, perhaps a building that houses another government agency within the jurisdiction. A virtual EOC is an exception to a physical EOC.

Emergency Operations Plan (EOP): A plan for responding to a variety of potential hazards.

Emergency Support Functions (ESF): An organized grouping of the governmental, private sector, and NGO capabilities and services that are most likely to be necessary for managing domestic incidents.

Essential Elements Of Information (EEI): Important and standard information items supporting timely and informed decisions.

Family Educational Rights and Privacy Act (FERPA): The Family Educational Rights and Privacy Act (FERPA) is a federal law that protects the privacy of student education records. It applies to every school that receives funds under the U.S. Department of Education.

Full-Scale Exercise (FSE): A complex, multiagency, multi-jurisdictional, and multidiscipline exercise that simulates a real event to test and evaluate emergency management systems.

Functional Exercise (FE): An exercise typically focused on exercising plans, policies, procedures, and staff members involved in management, direction, command, and control functions.

General Staff: A group of incident personnel organized according to function and reporting to the IC or Unified Command. The ICS General Staff consists of the Operations Section Chief, Planning Section Chief (PSC), Logistics Section Chief and Finance/Administration Section Chief.

Geographic Information Systems (GIS): A framework for gathering, managing, and analyzing data rooted in the science of geography. GIS analyzes spatial location and organizes layers of information into visualizations such as maps and 3D scenes, providing deeper insights into patterns, relationships, and situations.

Hazard: Something potentially dangerous or harmful; often the root cause of an unwanted outcome.

Health Insurance Portability and Accountability Act (HIPAA): The Health Insurance Portability and Accountability Act of 1996 (HIPAA) is a federal law that safeguards sensitive patient health information from being disclosed without the patient's consent or knowledge.

Homeland Security Exercise and Evaluation Program (HSEEP): A set of guiding principles for exercise programs, as well as a common approach to exercise program management, design, development, conduct, evaluation, and improvement planning.

Incident: An occurrence, natural or human caused, that necessitates a response to protect life or property. In this document, *incident* includes planned events as well as emergencies and disasters of all kinds and sizes.

Incident Action Plan (IAP): An oral or written plan containing the IC's or Unified Command's objectives and addressing tactics and support activities for the planned operational period, generally 12–24 hours.

Incident Command: The ICS organizational element responsible for overall management of the incident and consisting of the IC or Unified Command and any additional activated Command Staff.

Incident Commander (IC): The individual responsible for on-scene incident activities, including developing incident objectives and ordering and releasing resources. The IC has overall authority and responsibility for conducting incident operations.

Incident Command Post (ICP): The field location where staff perform the primary functions of incident command. The ICP may be co-located with the incident base or other incident facilities.

Incident Command System (ICS): A standardized approach to the command, control and coordination of on-scene incident management, providing a common hierarchy within which personnel from multiple organizations can work. ICS brings procedures, personnel, facilities, equipment and communications into a common organizational structure to aid in the management of on-scene resources during incidents. ICS applies to small, large, and complex incidents of all kinds, including planned events.

Individualized Education Plans (IEP): School districts must provide an IEP for all students receiving special education services.

Institution of Higher Education (IHE): A postsecondary college, university, or institution. They may be public, private, two-year, and four-year institutions. Interoperability: The ability of systems, personnel, and equipment to provide and receive functionality, data, information and/or services to and from other systems, personnel, and equipment, between both public and private agencies, departments, and other organizations, in a manner enabling them to operate effectively together. It allows emergency management/ response personnel and their affiliated organizations to communicate within and across agencies and jurisdictions via voice, data, or video-on-demand, in real time, when needed, and when authorized.

Incident Management: The broad spectrum of activities and organizations providing operations, coordination, and support at all levels of government, using both governmental and nongovernmental resources to plan for, respond to, and recover from an incident, regardless of cause, size, or complexity.

Incident Objective: A statement of a desired incident outcome. Incident objectives drive strategies and tactics. Incident objectives should be realistic, achievable, and measurable, yet flexible enough to allow strategic and tactical alternatives.

Intelligence/Investigations Function: The effort to determine the source or cause of an incident (for example, disease outbreak, fire, complex coordinated attack or cyber incident) in order to control its impact and help prevent the occurrence of similar incidents. In ICS, this function may belong to the Planning Section, Operations Section, Command Staff or General Staff (as a separate section) or to a combination of these entities.

Interoperability: The ability of systems, personnel and equipment to exchange functionality, data, information, and services with other systems, personnel and equipment—among public and private agencies, departments, and other organizations—in a manner enabling them to operate effectively together.

Jeanne Clery Disclosure of Campus Security Policy and Campus Crime Statistics Act (Clery Act): Federal law that outlines requirements for IHEs participating in the Title IV Higher Education Act Federal student assistance programs regarding campus crime statistics and security information disclosures.

Joint Field Office (JFO): The primary federal incident management field structure. The JFO is a temporary federal facility that provides a central location for the coordination of SLTT and federal governments, private sector organizations, and NGOs that have primary responsibility for response and recovery.

Joint Information Center (JIC): A facility in which personnel coordinate incident-related public information activities. The JIC serves as the central POC for all news media. Public Information Officers (PIO) from all participating agencies colocate in, or coordinate virtually through, the JIC.

Joint Information System (JIS): A structure that integrates overarching incident information and public affairs into a cohesive organization designed to provide consistent, coordinated, accurate, accessible, timely, and complete information during crisis or incident operations.

Jurisdiction: Jurisdiction has two definitions depending on the context:

- **A range or sphere of authority:** Public agencies have jurisdiction at an incident related to their legal responsibilities and authority. Jurisdictional authority at an incident can be political or geographical (for example, SLTT or federal boundary lines) or functional (for example, law enforcement or public health).

- A political subdivision (for example, municipal, county, parish, state or federal) with the responsibility to ensure public safety, health and welfare within its legal authorities and geographic boundaries.

Liaison Officer: A member of the ICS Command Staff responsible for coordinating with representatives from cooperating and assisting agencies or organizations.

Logistics Section: The ICS section responsible for providing facilities, services, and material support for an incident.

Management by Objectives: A management approach fundamental to NIMS that involves (1) establishing objectives (specific, measurable, and realistic outcomes to be achieved); (2) identifying strategies, tactics, and tasks designed to achieve the objectives; (3) performing the tactics and tasks, and measuring and documenting results; and (4) taking corrective action to modify strategies, tactics and performance to achieve the objectives.

Mitigation: The capabilities necessary to reduce the loss of life and property by lessening the impacts of natural and human-caused disasters, incidents, and events.

Multiagency Coordination Group (MAC Group): A group, typically consisting of agency administrators or organization executives or their designees, that provides policy guidance to incident personnel, supports resource prioritization and allocation, and enables decision-making among elected and appointed officials, senior executives from other organizations and those directly responsible for incident management.

Mutual Aid Agreement Or Assistance Agreement: A written or oral agreement between and among agencies/organizations and jurisdictions that provides a mechanism for quickly obtaining assistance in the form of personnel, equipment, materials, and other associated services. The primary objective is to facilitate the rapid, short-term deployment of support prior to, during, and after an incident.

National Association of School Psychologists (NASP): The National Association of School Psychologists is a national professional organization for school psychologists.

National Association of School Resource Officers (NASRO): The National Association of School Resource Officers (NASRO) provides training to school-based law enforcement officers.

National Incident Management System (NIMS): A systematic, proactive approach for guiding all levels of government, NGOs and the private sector to work together to prevent, protect against, mitigate, respond to, and recover from the effects of incidents. NIMS provides stakeholders across the whole community with the shared vocabulary, systems and processes to successfully deliver the capabilities described in the National Preparedness System. NIMS provides a consistent foundation for dealing with all incidents, from daily occurrences to those requiring a coordinated federal response.

National Preparedness Goal (NPG): Doctrine describing what it means for the whole community to be prepared for the types of incidents that pose the greatest threat to national security, including acts of terrorism, emergencies, and disasters, regardless of cause. The goal reads, "A secure and resilient Nation with the capabilities required across the whole community to prevent, protect against, mitigate, respond to and recover from the threats and hazards that pose the greatest risk."

National Response Coordination Center (NRCC): A multiagency coordination center located at FEMA headquarters. Its staff coordinates the overall federal support for major disasters and emergencies, including catastrophic incidents and emergency management program implementation. The NRCC also houses the NBEOC.

National Response Framework (NRF): A guide for the nation's response to all types of disasters and emergencies. It is built on NIMS concepts for aligning key roles and responsibilities. It includes the ESFs.

National Threat Assessment Center (NTAC): The National Threat Assessment Center (NTAC) is part of the U.S. Secret Service. The NTAC provides research and best practices for preventing targeted acts of violence.

Nongovernmental Organization (NGO): A nonprofit group that is based on the interests of its members, individuals, or institutions. An NGO is not created by a government, but it may work cooperatively with government. Examples of NGOs include faith-based groups, relief agencies, organizations that support people with access and functional needs (AFN) and animal welfare organizations.

Operational Period: The time scheduled for executing a given set of operation actions, as the IAP specifies. Operational periods can vary in length but are typically 12–24 hours.

Operational Security: Implementing procedures and activities to protect sensitive or classified operations involving sources and methods of intelligence collection, investigative techniques, tactical actions, countersurveillance measures, counterintelligence methods, undercover officers, cooperating witnesses and informants.

Operations Section: The ICS section responsible for implementing tactical incident operations described in the IAP. The Operations Section may include subordinate branches, divisions, and groups.

Plain Language: Communication that the intended audience can understand and that meets the communicator's purpose. For the purpose of NIMS, plain language refers to a communication style that avoids or limits the use of codes, abbreviations, and jargon during incidents involving more than one agency.

Planning Section: The ICS section that collects, evaluates, and disseminates operational information related to an incident and helps prepare and document the IAP. This section also maintains information on the current and forecasted situation and on the status of assigned resources.

position qualifications: The minimum criteria necessary for individuals to fill a specific position.

Position Task Book (PTB): A document identifying the competencies, behaviors, and tasks that personnel should demonstrate to become qualified for a defined incident management or support position.

Private Sector: Organizations and individuals that are not part of a governmental structure. The private sector includes for-profit and not-for-profit organizations, formal and informal structures, commerce, and industry.

Protocol: A set of established guidelines for action (applying to individuals, teams, functions, or capabilities) under various specified conditions.

Public Information Officer (PIO): A member of the ICS Command Staff responsible for interfacing with the public, the media, and other agencies that have incident-related information needs.

Readiness & Emergency Management for Schools (REMS): The Readiness and Emergency Management for Schools (REMS) Technical Assistance Center supports U.S. schools with developing, implementing, and maintaining emergency operations plans (EOPs).

Reunification Exercise: A school reunification exercise brings the district, its schools, and community together to be trained on parent-student reunification.

Reunification Site: This is typically an off-site location where schools evacuate. Examples include churches, recreation centers, athletic facilities, meeting halls, movie theaters.

Risk Assessment: Districts and schools should conduct school safety risk assessments to evaluate potential vulnerabilities and risks in their schools.

Rescue Task Force (RTF): A group of trained individuals who work together to provide emergency medical care and move victims to safety

Safety Officer: In ICS, a member of the Command Staff responsible for monitoring incident operations and advising the IC or Unified Command on all matters relating to operational safety, including the health and safety of incident personnel. The Safety Officer modifies or stops the work of personnel to prevent unsafe acts.

Section: The ICS organizational element having responsibility for a major functional area of incident management (Operations, Planning, Logistics, or Finance/Administration); capitalized when part of an official name.

Site Assessment: An information collection tool that examines the safety, security, accessibility, and emergency preparedness of buildings and grounds. This is one source of information when the planning team is identifying threats and hazards.

Situation Report: Confirmed or verified information regarding the details of an incident.

Span Of Control: The number of subordinates for which a supervisor is responsible, usually expressed as a ratio of supervisors to individuals.

Staging Area: A temporary location for available resources in which personnel, supplies and equipment await operational assignment.

Standard Operating Procedure: A reference document or operations manual that provides the purpose, authorities, duration and details for the preferred method of performing a single function or several interrelated functions in a uniform manner.

Standard Response Protocol (SRP): The Standard Response Protocol is from The "I Love U Guys" Foundation. The protocol describes emergency response actions for various school-related emergencies, from severe weather, bomb threats, to an active shooter.

Standard Reunification Method (SRM): From The "I Love U Guys" Foundation, this school emergency protocol provides proven methods for K–12 schools to plan, practice, and complete parent-student reunification.

School Resource Officer (SRO): The National Association of School Resource Officers (NASRO) defines an SRO as "a carefully selected, specifically trained, and properly equipped full-time law enforcement officer with sworn law enforcement authority." They are trained in school-based law enforcement and emergency response and are typically armed, unless prohibited by law.

School Climate: The school climate is based on the learning environment and relationships between staff, teachers, counselors, students, and other community members.

Student Information System (SIS): A student information system (SIS) collects and stores school-wide data, including staff, guardian, and student data, and makes it accessible to the appropriate school and district staff. SIS data includes information like names, birthdates, addresses, and class rosters.

Tabletop Exercise: A discussion-based session where participants work together to respond to simulated emergency situations.

Targeted Violence: This is premeditated violence that is directed toward a specific target.

Task Force: Any combination of resources of different kinds and types assembled to support a specific mission or operational need; capitalized when part of an official name.

Terrorism: Any activity involving an act (1) that is dangerous to human life or potentially destructive of critical infrastructure and is a violation of the criminal laws of the United States or of any state or other subdivision of the United States and (2) that appears to be intended to intimidate or coerce a civilian population, or to influence the policy of a government by intimidation or coercion, or to affect the conduct of a government by mass destruction, assassination, or kidnapping.

Threat: A natural or human-caused occurrence, an individual, an entity, or an action having or indicating the potential to harm life, information, operations, property, or the environment.

Threat Assessment: This process involves assessing risk from a specific threat.

Threat Assessment Team: An internal, multidisciplinary team who evaluates, investigates, and analyzes potential threats to school safety.

Unified Command: An ICS command structure that applies when more than one agency has incident jurisdiction or when incidents cross political jurisdictions.

Unity of Command: A NIMS guiding principle stating that each individual involved in incident management reports to and takes direction from only one person.

About the Authors

Dr. David E. Johnson is a lifelong educator and certificated school administrator with extensive experience leading safety programs at the building and district levels. A decorated U.S. Air Force veteran, he also directed Emergency Management and Defense Support of Civil Authorities programs, blending military expertise with educational leadership.

Glenn G. Norling, MA, is a retired FBI Special Agent and Executive Director of the Active Shooter Prevention Project. A certified crisis manager and court-designated expert on school emergency drills, he has trained thousands nationwide, advancing safety, preparedness, and resilience in schools and communities through decades of real-world experience.

Dr. Pamela M. VanHorn is a leadership and school improvement consultant with 27 years in K–12 education. She has served in leadership, evaluator, and educator roles with universities and the Ohio Department of Education, dedicated to improving student achievement and creating safe, supportive school environments.

Chief Jeffrey Yarbrough, MS, CPM, is a 30-year police veteran and Chief of the Hutto Police Department in Texas. A nationally recognized school safety expert, he led two ISD police departments, including one serving 51,000 students, created an award-winning safety model, and authored Redefining School Safety and Policing: A Transformative Four Pillar Model.

Shaun Hurtado, MA, brings 20 years of experience as a teacher, coach, administrator, and consultant across TK–12 schools in urban, rural, and suburban communities. He presents at conferences statewide, coaches administrators and consults with districts, focusing on leadership development, positive school culture, student mental health, and restorative practices.